INTELLE __
AND
ACTION

For the student members, past and present,
of the Research Institute in Systematic Theology

INTELLECT
AND
ACTION

Elucidations on Christian
Theology and the Life of Faith

Colin E. Gunton

T&T CLARK
EDINBURGH

T&T CLARK LTD
59 GEORGE STREET
EDINBURGH EH2 2LQ
SCOTLAND

www.tandtclark.co.uk

First published 2000

ISBN 0 567 08735 2

British Library Cataloguing-in-Publication Data
A catalogue record for this book is available from the British Library

Typeset by Fakenham Photosetting Limited, Fakenham, Norfolk
Printed and bound in Great Britain by Bookcraft, Midsomer Norton

CONTENTS

PREFACE

Seven of the papers in this collection have been written in the last eighteen months, and represent a continuing project of thought, not in a linear way, as if one builds on the one before, but as an attempt to enrich and develop earlier trains of thought. The set begins with two on the nature, first of dogma – as concentration of the Church's public teaching – and then of systematic theology. They naturally lead into a third, which attempts to explore some of the many ramifications of Christian claims to know. The fourth moves beyond the intellectual into the realm of action, or at least of talking about it. Repeating, in its opening pages, some of the opening themes of the discussion of systematic theology, it moves to ask, in conversation with Kierkegaard and Barth above all, what bearing theology so conceived might have on theological ethics. Papers which follow examine concepts of theological ethics: holiness, a concept taken directly from Scripture, and then virtue, one borrowed from the Greeks and currently much in vogue.

The four final chapters are devoted to an examination of aspects of the relation between divine action and human response. The exercises known as 'dogma' and 'theology' form part of the human response to what we summarise with such terms as creation, election, salvation and revelation: all those actions and events we describe as divine grace. In that human response, the work of the intellect is a moral action, in that respect differing not at all from those enterprises which are more explicitly ethical. Where they do differ is in emphasis, with, though far too schematically, dogmatic theology conceived as a response to revelation, theological ethics to election and atonement. And so papers on election and salvation follow, both of them in part explorations of the legacy of Calvin, whose often warm, affirmative, lucidly intellectual, and for the most part open thought is rightly receiving attention at this time when it has become an ecumenical responsibility to explore the particularities of our heritage.

Indeed, as I have reread the papers in order to remove any unnecessary repetition, I have realised how many of them contain major appropriations of the thought of this theologian. It becomes more and more borne upon me that his is one of the great minds of the tradition, hugely underestimated almost everywhere for all kinds of bad reasons, some but by no means all due to that movement called 'Calvinism'. R. J. Neuhaus perhaps puts his finger on the real cause, that secular thought attacks Calvin relentlessly in order to discourage people from considering the alternative he offers.[1]

The other two papers devoted to response are concerned with that stumbling block of the modern age, freedom. The Christian gospel is an offer of freedom which is often accused of being the opposite. In response to that, it could be argued – and it is part of the argument of these papers – that, by adopting the doctrine that freedom is freedom from God and our neighbour, the modern world has entered a slavery far greater than that ever experienced in the Christian era. Yet that would be too easy, for it must also be acknowledged that by virtue of her deficient hold on what it means to speak of the grace of God the Father mediated through Christ and the Holy Spirit, the Church is by no means innocent of being a leading cause of the gospel's rejection by many of the leading thinkers of the modern world. Freedom, it can be observed, is that which characterises – or fails to characterise – human action, and it is perhaps these final chapters which might be considered to justify the otherwise rather ambitious second pole of the title. As such, they will also provide an introduction for a future selection of papers on *Modern Questions*, though, it is to be hoped, not quite in the manner of those publishers who print the first chapter of the next thriller at the end of the current one.

In the dedication of his great commentary on Leviticus to some of his students, Jacob Milgrom cites the following rabbinical text: 'I have learned much from my teachers, more from my colleagues, but from my students more than all.' That is my belief also. Among the highlights of my endlessly

---

[1] R. J. Neuhaus, *The Naked Public Square* (Grand Rapids: Eerdman, 2nd edition, 1986), p. 175.

rewarding life as a theologian are the weekly seminars, and sometimes longer conferences, of the Research Institute in Systematic Theology at King's College, begun and still supported by my dear friend and colleague, Christoph Schwöbel, now of the University of Heidelberg. Many of these papers were first, and certainly second, heard by, and usually improved with the help of, that enthusiastic and intelligent group of colleagues and students, only some of whom will be named in the footnotes. Indeed, what better compliment could a teacher be paid than that the students have during the last four summer vacations continued to meet and confer week by week? I must thank Paul Metzger for being the begetter of these occasions, but also Peter Robinson, Mark Patterson and Shirley Martin, who have carried on the tradition. Finally, particular thanks must go to my daughter, Carolyn, who has meticulously checked the proofs and supplied the indexes.

Colin Gunton
King's College, London, June 2000

CHAPTER 1

DOGMA, THE CHURCH AND THE TASK OF THEOLOGY[1]

The thesis to be defended in this chapter is advanced with the aid of a metaphor: that, so far as the relations of dogma to theology are concerned, dogma is that which delimits the garden of theology, providing a space in which theologians may play freely and cultivate such plants as are cultivable in the space which is so defined. As soon as that is said, however, it must be qualified, and the chapter will largely consist of a rehearsal of the qualifications. But the general point is that just as a garden is not a garden without some boundaries – or just as the created world is only what it is as a work of God because it is finite in space and time – so theology ceases to be Christian theology if it effectively ceases to remain true to its boundaries. So far as the relation between dogma and theology is concerned, the metaphor enables us to concentrate on one central matter, namely, the way by which the boundaries of theology are set: we might say, the rules within which theology operates. It follows from this that much depends upon what the Church, which effectively defines dogma, does and thinks it is doing in laying down dogmatic definitions, so that the bulk of our discussion will be concerned with dogma as a function of the Church.

To be sure, at least two further things are necessary for such an account to be developed. The first is recognition of the fact

---

[1] Prepared for a conference of the Australian Theological forum, 'The Task of Theology Today', Brisbane, July 1997, and published in its proceedings, *The Task of Theology Today. Doctrines and Dogmas*, ed. Victor Pfitzner and Hilary Regan (Edinburgh: T. & T. Clark, 1999), pp. 1–22. First published in *Neue Zeitschrift für Systematische Theologie und Religionsphilosophie* 40 (1998), 66–79.

that while theology may operate within the garden marked out by dogma, its activities may also come to change both the territory and the character of the garden. This raises the question of authority. What is the authority of the theologian in the Church? How far can and should theological activity alter the boundaries of the garden, as it undoubtedly has done and does? The situation is most clearly illustrated by Hans Küng's difference with the papal authorities, but there are necessarily, if less clear, instances in all churches. And the second requirement is the biblical and eschatological proviso attendant on all dogmatic activity, whether engaged in by church bodies or particular theologians: that all theological activity is subject to the test of Scripture and the judgement of the age to come. Here is raised the question not of the authority of Church and theology, but of the status of them both. What truth is claimable this side of eternity by fallible and sinful human beings, if they all are fallible, as some but not all churches believe?

In both of these respects we are concerned with pneumatology, with what we believe the eschatological Spirit to enable within the constraints of time and history, and how his gifts are distributed. Whatever else is decided, it should surely be agreed that, if there is to be a place for dogma in the Church, its function is at once both to delimit and to realise theology's freedom. This freedom is the freedom of theologians to respond to the Holy Spirit's inspiration in seeking to feed the Church and engage the world. If the boundaries are too restrictive, the expression of the truth for today will be impeded; if too vague or absent altogether, other masters will rule than the gospel, and the garden will become a desert. The historical and theological difficulties which face us are exacerbated by the differences between the churches in their understanding of dogma, and these will inevitably shape much of the discussion.

I   *Something on origins and history*

As is well known, the word 'dogma' has many meanings, from its original meaning of 'opinion', through its classical theological sense of ecclesiastical definition, to the pejorative modern sense it has acquired since the Enlightenment. Arguments from etymology are of little use in themselves, but it is relevant to note that the original use of the word 'dogma' to mean 'opinion' survived fairly late into the history of theology. In the words of Isidore of Seville, 'the last Western church Father', a dogma signifies: *Hoc puto esse bonum, hoc puto esse verum,* perhaps best rendered, 'I judge this to be good, this to be true'.[2] That continues to be important in a situation in which it may be suspected that some church authorities may appear to place their own pronouncements too much at the other end of the scale, claiming for them the kind of certainty that might appear to breach the eschatological limits of all human words. But this is not the sense which interests us now, which is rather the signification the word has acquired through time to refer, generally, to the official teaching of the Church as an institution. It is that word 'official' which is at the centre. There are, of course, degrees and varieties of the official, and in them lies the theological difficulty and interest of the subject. Here I shall concentrate on two, and explain their difference and relation by means of a historical claim: that in one of the senses of the word 'dogma', theology begins in dogma; in another, theology enables dogma to come into being.

The first sense is to be found in Irenaeus' contention that there is, in the churches of his period, a shared and universal confession of faith. Technically we are in the realm of confession rather than dogma, yet these confessions are a form of dogma by virtue of the fact that they are the utterances of a community or institution rather than of unrelated individuals. This confession is articulated by Irenaeus in a number of places, and is not verbally identical in all of them. But he clearly thinks he is articulating the same shared content. That is to say, there is in these appeals to the rule of faith a relative plurality of verbal forms within a recognisable unity of content. This doctrinal confession makes Irenaeus' theology possible – it gives him a space in which to operate – for it is the defence of the confession against the threat of heresy which both empowers and provides an intellectual framework for his

[2] U. Wickert, 'Dogma I. Historisch', *Theologische Realenzyklopädie* 9, p. 29.

systematic defence of the catholic faith against Gnosticism.
And, to refer to an earlier point, it frees him: frees him to say
things about God's creation and redemption of the world
which edify – build up – the Church to this day. If he is telling
the truth, it suggests that a generally shared dogmatic content
is to be found in the Church of the late second century, even
though its implications have not yet been worked through.

Here we should pause to give an airing to two observations
which help to clarify what we are doing. The first is Eilert
Herms' recent contention that the function of dogma is the
articulation of the whole.[3] That is to say, dogma aims to articulate the universal implications of the Christian faith. The
notion derives, he says, from the Stoa, and, if we are to
circumvent the barrier modern conditions present to giving the
notion a fair hearing, we must realise that it is equivalent to the
German *Weltanschauung*[4] or Heidegger's *Daseinsverständnis*.[5]
Thus it is that Origen, the first to give a secure definition to the
idea, held that the dogma of the Church was the true
philosophy.[6] Clearly, that is something of what Irenaeus is
seeking, even though the philosophers were more of a problem
for him than they were for Origen. In opposition to the claims
of the Gnostics, he spells out in summary form the implications
of the Christian faith for our knowledge of God's action in
creation, reconciliation and redemption, to use Barth's characterisation of the originating, saving and eschatological
dimensions of God's acts in and toward the world. It is to be
observed that these adumbrations of the whole are not philosophical abstractions – as might be suggested by Herms'
likening of dogma to a world-view – for their point is right
human living in the Church and the world, as, again, the form
of Irenaeus' summaries makes clear. Moreover, dogmas claim
universality as an account of God, the world and human life
within it, but in a rather different way from *Weltanschauung* and

---

[3] Eilert Herms, 'Ganzheit als Geschick. Dogmatik als Begriff menschlicher
Ganzheitserfahrung und Anleitung zu ihrer Wahrnehmung', *Der Ganze
Mensch. Perspectiven lebensgeschichtlicher Individualität* (Berlin: de Gruyter, 1997),
pp. 369–405.
[4] Herms, 'Ganzheit als Geschick', p. 370.
[5] Herms, 'Ganzheit als Geschick', p. 372.
[6] Herms, 'Ganzheit als Geschick', p. 373, citing *Princ* 4. 1, *Cels* 1. 7, 3. 39.

Daseinsverständnis, because they remain essentially confessions of faith. In *that* sense, they never lose their character as 'opinion'. There is a necessary provisionality about all formulations which derives from their character.

The second observation is that of T. F. Torrance, who draws a strong, perhaps rather Platonic, distinction between dogma and dogmas.

> In *dogma* we are concerned with the one ultimate ground and creative source of the understanding and existence of the Church in the communication and self-giving of God's own Being ... In *dogmas,* however, we are concerned with the Church's historical inquiry and formulations of its knowledge of the fundamental *datum* of divine revelation as it is communicated in the Incarnation ...[7]

Torrance is here drawing on Barth's distinction between the reality of dogma itself and its expression in speech, and betrays a characteristically modern conception of the relativity of words to their time and context. People of different eras can use the same words and mean differently by them, as can perhaps be illustrated by the modern difficulty with the substance language of the creeds. Yet as Irenaeus' example again reminds us, for him it was identity of content, not of verbal form, that was intended in his summaries of universal Church teaching.

Underlying Torrance's distinction between dogma and dogmas is a conviction that there can only be dogma if there is revelation. Rahner has pointed out that for a modernism which rejects revelation, '"Dogma" expresses man's experience of himself in his religious indigence and only in that way something of the "divine"'.[8] But the rejection of the modernist denial of revelation does not imply that Torrance's is necessarily the best way to express the situation.[9] It seems more

---

[7] T. F. Torrance, *Theological Science* (Oxford: Oxford University Press, 1969), pp. 344–5; reissued Edinburgh: T. & T. Clark: 1996.

[8] Karl Rahner, 'Dogma', *The Concise Sacramentum Mundi* (New York: Seabury Press, 1975), p. 354.

[9] I shall not discuss further the question of the post-Kantian denial of the possibility of revelation because it would require a different chapter altogether. To demonstrate that this is not an evasion of the question, may I refer to my discussion of revelation in *A Brief Theology of Revelation. The 1993 Warfield Lectures* (Edinburgh: T. & T. Clark, 1995)?

illuminating to draw the line between the kerygma, or saving proclamation of the truth of the transmitted gospel, as classically in 1 Corinthians 15.3ff., and the dogma which is its concentration into teaching. That there is no absolute division between the two is shown by the fact that Irenaeus' summaries of the rule of faith are in many respects somewhere between the two. But that there is a distinction is shown by Herms' observation that with dogma we reach a kind of intellectual universalising of the truth claims of the gospel which goes beyond the Bible's kerygmatic and more occasional confessions of belief.

In Irenaeus there begins the process of giving intellectual articulation to the dogmatic claims of the primitive rule of faith, and it takes us to the second and formally ecclesiastical sense of the word 'dogma'. It is at this place that the qualification of Herms' analogy with world-views should be recalled, for alike in the scriptural summaries of the gospel, in Irenaeus' characterisation of the rule of faith and in later formal church symbols, the element of confession is never absent, at least so far as the great ecumenical creeds of the early centuries are concerned. Accordingly, the second sense of the word 'dogma' arises out of the theological endeavours of Irenaeus and his successors, and it is what can be called dogma proper, insofar as that represents the official teaching of the Church articulated in agreed propositional – though still confessional – form. The creeds of the ecumenically shared seven ecumenical councils are accordingly models of what is meant by dogma, though it should not be restricted to them. They respond to the theological controversies recorded in the writings of the early theologians and summarise the Church's response to them.

It is here, of course, that our path becomes tortuous, for there is little else that can be said which is likely to find ecumenical agreement. The reason is that it is generally agreed that dogma is a way of speaking of the official teaching of the Church or churches; but about the nature and authority of that teaching there are great differences, both between East and West and within the West. There are at least two interrelated questions here which have been bequeathed to us in the form that they have by the history of church disunity: authority and development. To the intrinsic difficulties sketched in the introductory paragraphs are added the complications attendant on human sin. There can be widespread agreement about the view that dogma in some way or other defines the teaching of the Church. But what specifically counts as approved dogma, how it comes to be approved, and the way in which the confessing community claims and exercises authority in the matter of its teaching are all matters of widespread disagreement. This is nowhere better illustrated than by the questions addressed by Newman on his route from Canterbury to Rome, as they have been so clearly expounded by Owen Chadwick. On the one side was Newman's Tractarian past, whose commitment to the immutability of dogma became for historical reasons no longer tenable. (It would appear that this pretension to immutability continues to be the position of Eastern Orthodoxy, perhaps part of its appeal today to disaffected Anglo-Catholics.) On the other side was his Roman present, whither he was in part enabled to move with indirect assistance from modern organic metaphors of development, ironically owed to liberalism, as Chadwick points out. But it was only in part that Newman was so led, for the problem derived not simply from the discovery that dogma has a history but from disagreement about the nature of dogma, who has the right to decide what is dogma, and by what means.[10] We shall understand something of the underlying theological questions if we spend some time looking now at the problem of Christian dogma in general.

II   *Dogma, the Church and the theologian*

The distinctive character of Christian dogma is that it affects to express divine mysteries – by which, after the example of the Letter to the Ephesians, I mean things *made known* – in human words, sometimes fairly confident human words. As in all theology, there are dangers to the left and the right of the path, though, as so often in politics also, extremes of left and right amount to very much the same thing. On the one hand there is the danger – at once the Neoplatonist and Kantian

[10] Owen Chadwick, *From Bossuet to Newman. The Birkbeck Lectures, 1955–6* (Cambridge: Cambridge University Press, 1957).

temptation – of rendering the God who makes known the mysteries so 'transcendent' of the words that they become simply projections; and on the other, of too closely identifying the words of the dogma with the Word of God. Both turn dogma into a merely or largely human work or achievement, whether of the theologian as virtuoso – in one Freudian slip I once heard, as prima madonna – playing autonomously on the instruments of reason and imagination, or of the Church too confidently realising eschatological finality. Both run the risk of either bypassing or depotentiating the one mediator of divine truth in action, Jesus Christ: that is, of ignoring the human mediation and eschatological orientation of all theological speech.

While the latter vice – of subordinating to the word of the all too human Church the biblical witness to Jesus – is the sin of which Protestants tend to accuse Catholics, the former – of denying the historical mediation of divine truth and replacing it with the theologian's more or less confident articulation of contemporary experience – is the far greater offence committed by modernism, whether Protestant or Catholic. This is because at one and the same time it denies to God the capacity to mediate truth historically – through this historically crucified, raised and ascended human being – and deprives human rationality of the capacity to be enabled by the Spirit to articulate the truth of revelation and so speak the Word of God. Modernism is the paradoxical outcome of Kant's strongly dualist view of the relation of God and human minds, and forgets the reality and the necessity of revelation as gift. God's supposed inaccessibility becomes the occasion effectively to replace dogma with descriptions of experience purportedly licensed by modern conditions. Kantian dogma – dogma in the derived and secondary sense of an all-encompassing world-view tending to subjectivism and idealism and before which even the gospel must be judged – displaces dogma as the summary expression of revealed mystery.

It is surely significant that it was as he emerged from his early Kantianism that Barth moved towards a reappropriation of something like the classical conception of dogma. He shared the Neoprotestant suspicion of dogmas too confidently claiming knowledge of divine things. 'The Word of God is above dogma as the heavens are above the earth.'[11] That strong distinction between the Word and dogma – between all human words and the Word of God – in effect repeats Luther's assertion that it is Scripture, not churchly approval, which serves as a criterion of the truth of dogma, and *could* lead to the very transcendentalism of which we are speaking. But it is certainly not the main point of Barth's strong distinction, which is to lay the ground for a more positive conception. He cites Isidore of Seville: *Articulus est perceptio divinae veritatis tendens in ipsam.* A paraphrase rather than a strict translation would say that a dogma expresses a conviction of divine truth which derives from an indwelling in that truth.[12]

It is the nature of the *tendens* or indwelling which concerns us, for it maintains a continuing relation of the words the Church uses to the God who may, or may not, continue to licence them. How may the Church so *indwell* divine truth that her words express the truth of the gospel? It is here that Eastern Orthodoxy, however rigid it can sometimes be in both appearance and reality, has a broader conception of the matter than much of the Western tradition, because it seeks to root the expression of dogma not in a teaching office but in a not always clearly demarcated appeal to a broad range of authorities: Church, Scripture, tradition and the seven ecumenical councils. In some way or other, dogma represents the confession of the whole Christian community, its Scriptures and its tradition in the whole sweep of its life, especially including worship. Contrast this with the more negative understanding of the function of dogma as a wall against heresy found in some Western understandings after Augustine.[13]

Yet there are equal and opposite difficulties to face. A position which, apparently, refuses *in principle*, and not because the Church is now divided, to countenance the possibility of an elaboration of dogma beyond the seven ecumenical councils appears to rule out not only the action of the Spirit in the Church but also historical developments which appear to

[11] Karl Barth, *Church Dogmatics*, translation edited by G. W. Bromiley and T. F. Torrance (Edinburgh: T. & T. Clark, 1957–1975), 1/1, p. 266.
[12] Barth, *Church Dogmatics* 1/1, p. 267.
[13] Wickert, 'Dogma I. Historisch', p. 29.

be theologically justified. What, for example, are we to make of the decision of the Fourth Lateran Council of 1215 to define the dogma of creation out of nothing?[14] The circumstances of its promulgation are of classic form. A threat to Christian truth arising from the renewed circulation of Aristotelian doctrines of the eternity of the world is met by the properly dogmatic reassertion of teaching going back at least as far as Irenaeus. While neither Eastern Orthodox nor orthodox Protestants should have difficulty with the *content* of such a decree, for it is a republication of long-standing teaching and was reaffirmed by the Reformation, its status is surely in doubt as far as the East is concerned, and not only for reasons of church order, because it is not, at least with respect to the means used to promulgate it, the teaching of the universal Church.

If it is indeed held for reasons other than those of church disunity that there can be no new developments beyond the patristic period, that would appear for biblical and pneumatological reasons to be too restrictive. Jesus Christ may be personally and revelationally final, but that does not appear to rule out new expressions of what revelation implies in different historical contexts. Rome and Reformation have in different ways affirmed the necessity of new dogmatic confession. Corresponding to the former's promulgation of the immaculate conception and the infallibility of the pope is the latter's employment of confessions. The functions of such dogmas in the two movements are chiastically different. On the one hand, the Roman formulations tend, certainly insofar as they are justified in Newman's terms, to be 'progressive', as the new drawing out of implications of the original idea of Christianity, while they are at the same time promulgated in highly 'conservative' ecclesiastical terms. On the other hand, the Reformation confessions often purport to be restoring lost elements of the original gospel while legislating for a changed church-political situation. These confessions, as well as Barmen in 1934, show that the post-Reformation confession has become a kind of alternative form of authoritative dogma to what had, for the Reformers, become the problematic form of the Roman

---

[14] Paul Haffner, *Mystery of Creation* (Leominster: Gracewing, 1995), p. 30.

approach.[15] Yet the fact remains that both Roman and Reformation formulations are in different ways innovatory as statements of dogma.

When new doctrines are added, or when new forms of dogma are sought to answer to new historical crises – and in that respect, both Roman and Reformation formulations are very similar in function to the symbols of the seven ecumenical councils – by what criteria do churches judge whether this is the same gospel? What in particular are the criteria of identity which give reasons for concluding that it is the same faith which is being summarised and defended? They cannot be discussed in detail here, for we are concerned chiefly with the relation between dogma and theology. But they reach to the heart of our first consideration of this question, the theologian's involvement with dogma, both historical and systematic. The theologian is *directly* involved in dogma as one putatively learned enough in both historical and systematic theology to be able to consider the broader context within which dogmatic formulation takes shape, and so to assist the Church as a whole to make informed decisions.

The first question within such a purview concerns the relation of dogma to Scripture. In asserting dogma's subordination to Scripture, we see that part of its point is not the imposition of a narrow uniformity but of providing what can be called an intermediate measure. Scripture is not a monolithically uniform medium. Not only may the devil quote Scripture, but the diversity of the witness allows for an unforced – that is to say, not artificial – openness of theology to new needs and cultural contexts and thus for a relative freedom of interpretation for both theologian and preacher. The intermediate measure is that perilous enterprise called dogma: in which the teaching of Scripture is so summarised that both an oppressive

---

[15] The concept of dogma was sparingly used in the Middle Ages, on the grounds that the deposit of faith ruled out innovation: it could be understood in a new way (*nove*), though there could be no novelties (*nova*). See Wickert, 'Dogma I. Historisch', p. 30. It might be claimed, therefore, that the Reformation led to its renewal. For debates about the outcome of mediaeval discussion, up to and including Newman, see Chadwick, *From Bossuet to Newman*. Newman's position might have been more satisfactory had he not much of the time written as though he believed that anything coming from the Reformation was almost by definition wrong.

narrowness and a shapeless plurality are obviated. Here the theologian's task is to consider the relation between the two in broad context.[16]

Parallel to the question of the relation of dogma to Scripture is its orientation to tradition, and this enables us to focus the second side of the theologian's responsibility, which takes the form of a concern for systematic coherence. The Second Vatican Council attempted with some success to relativise the dispute about Scripture and tradition by referring both to the one divine revelation which founds them.[17] But the under-lying doubt – now brought out into the open – remains of whether some things promulgated by Rome as dogma do in effect betray a creativity of the Church which goes beyond the bounds set by Scripture's articulation of revelation. It is here that we realise that we cannot escape reference to a crucial task of the theologian, which is to question not only whether the Church has been too enthusiastically creative, but whether the results of such creativity can be seen to cohere with other articles of the faith as they have been accepted and handed down within the process of tradition. That is to say, part of theology's systematic task is to examine the coherence of different dogmatic expressions not only with Scripture but with one another. That is to say, further: it is not enough simply to accuse a church of excessive dogmatic creativity on narrowly scriptural grounds, or on scriptural grounds alone, because it is not easy to decide whether and in what sense a dogma – for instance, that of the virgin birth – is truly the expression of the witness of Scripture taken as a whole. Such doctrines must therefore be assessed also in terms of their systematic relations to other doctrines.

Now, by systematic I do not mean a concern with the merely logical relation of doctrines to each other as part of a system; in

[16] How much one can make of empirical observation in this matter is doubtful, but it is at least arguable that it is the loss of the dogmatic measure which has helped generate the undisciplined disorder that is modernist Protestantism – and not only that – while perhaps the excessive uniformity sometimes imposed by Rome has encouraged the rebelliousness of many theologians, a phenomenon without real parallel in Eastern Orthodoxy, with its relatively more open structures.

[17] 'Dogmatic Constitution on Divine Revelation', *Vatican Council II. The Conciliar and Post-Conciliar Documents*, edited by A. Flannery OP (Leominster: Fowler Wright, 1975), pp. 754–5.

fact, scarcely at all is that meant. As we have seen, the difference between dogmas and world-views is that the former remain confessions and therefore still to some degree 'opinions': acts of faith on the part of the Church whose coherence with one another and with Scripture can only be decided provisionally; that is to say, under eschatological proviso. On the other hand, we may have so loose a conception of systematicity that intellectual irresponsibility is encouraged. It is possible to hold that logic is not enough while at the same time failing to understand that the faith has its own logic, its overall coherence according to which believers and unbelievers, may, in different ways, be presented with the faith's claims to be true, both intellectually and morally. This is something of what is meant by 'systematic': a concern for the general coherence of what the church proclaims and the relative weighting of its various articles so that its bearing upon human life in the Church and the world may be made as patent as possible.[18]

One example of the way in which theological work bears upon the question of dogmatic definition is the doctrine of the *Filioque*, so important for the relations between East and West. Historically, it is a lamentable example of what happens when one branch of the Church develops dogma unilaterally. But the breach engendered can be healed only by patient theological work by theologians aware of the systematic differences lying deep within the intricacies of trinitarian theology and of theological history. As John Zizioulas and the working party of the British Council of Churches have alike argued, real questions for the life and worship of the Church and for the understanding of what it is to be a human being in the world are at stake.[19] True dogma is never merely dogmatic. Only as the broad systematic ramifications are understood and faced is there any likelihood that the differences of dogma can be

---

[18] The matter of weighting can be illustrated easily. If the dogma of creation is emphasised at the expense of salvation, or the reverse, the content of the faith as a whole comes under threat. A creation spirituality on its own is inadequately Christian, as is a gnosticising understanding of salvation as salvation out of the world.

[19] British Council of Churches, *The Forgotten Trinity, Volume 1, The Report of the BCC Study Commission on Trinitarian Doctrine Today* (London: British Council of Churches, 1989); John D. Zizioulas, *Being as Communion. Studies in Personhood and the Church* (London: Darton, Longman & Todd, 1985).

settled, and it is surely not without significance that some Western churches are already reconsidering the use of this expression in their creeds, partly as the result of theological work.

Let me, however, take another highly contentious article in order to illustrate the systematic questions involved in dogma. Karl Barth remarked that the one reason for not becoming a Roman Catholic was the analogy of being, and I share the reasons underlying his objection. But because the debate over that is replete with misunderstanding and obscurity, I shall take another example of importance not only within the West but between West and East. The dogma of the immaculate conception of the virgin Mary produces a rent in the doctrinal fabric, I would contend, because it both endangers the shape of salvation and leads to a whole range of other theological and ecclesial problems bound up with its failure to allow for an adequate conception of the humanity of the Saviour. (That is, of course, in addition to its extremely dubious biblical justification. As important for a child of the Reformation is the problematic relation of this dogma to Scripture. Unless a dogma can reasonably be claimed to serve as an interpretation of the teaching of Scripture as a whole, it is essentially problematic.)

To enlarge this contention, I shall appeal to the ancient slogan devised in opposition to all Apollinarianism, Eutychianism and monophysitism, 'the unassumed is the unhealed'. Is it the case that the dogma of the immaculate conception of Mary effectively means that the Saviour is screened from the real perils of our humanity, in the way that he is by Schleiermacher's equally objectionable contention that Jesus was not really tempted?[20] Thomas Weinandy has contended that it is not the case, unconvincingly, I believe, because if salvation is to be a truly human as well as divine victory over the evil that holds human life in thrall, we cannot affirm a dogma which makes it appear that the flesh Jesus bore was already in some way automatically immune from the sin

---

[20] F. D. E. Schleiermacher, *The Christian Faith*, translated by H. R. Mackintosh and J. S. Stewart (Edinburgh: T. & T. Clark, 1928), §93. 4: 'His development must be thought of as wholly free from everything which we have to conceive as conflict', p. 382.

and stain of that flesh which the rest of us bear.[21] Does it not rather elevate a double *cordon sanitaire* between Jesus' humanity and ours, leading to the allotting to Mary of a place in the scheme of redemption neither licensed by Scripture nor giving to one who was actually crucified his full mediating role?

For this latter to be realised, I believe, the Saviour must be bone of our bone and flesh of our flesh. He must indeed be sinless, and, indeed, free of taint. But if that freedom is to be mediated to us, he must also share to the full the conditions of our taint. For that, it is necessary for him to be constituted of the same stuff of which we are made, part of a created order, subjected to vanity and in need of redemption. The taint does not indeed touch him, in the sense that he offers his humanity, through the eternal Spirit, perfect to the Father. But it must be through the Spirit: that is to say, through the process of a life of real struggle and temptation, including a real temptation in Gethsemane to evade the implications of his human calling. What I am in effect claiming is that the dogma of the immaculate conception is inconsistent with the earlier ecumenical dogma of Chalcedon which affirmed the full humanity of Christ, *homoousios* with us in all things apart from sin.

I use that example because if we are to be open in ecumenical discussion, as in all dialogue about differences, we have to be absolutely honest about what divides us. And it brings me back to the point of dogma. Dogmas are rules, but like all rules they become oppressive if they do not fulfil two requirements. The first is that rules should not be multiplied beyond necessity; that is, they should be subjected to Ockham's razor. To see the necessity of this general principle, we have only to glance at modern government, whether of what is called left or right, whose mania for legislating the happiness of humanity has in almost all modern societies led to a kind of enslavement by bureaucracy. The question of whether it is the case that the dogma which I have attacked is necessary – even supposing that it might be true – takes us to the second requirement, which is that the rules should achieve that which they set out to do. In the case of an institution, let us say a

---

[21] Thomas Weinandy, *In the Likeness of Sinful Flesh. An Essay on the Humanity of Christ* (Edinburgh: T. & T. Clark), 1993, pp. 153–6.

school, rules are those features of its life which enable the ends
of the institution to be achieved without undue disturbance:
with, that is to say, the right combination of direction from
above and initiative from below. In our case, dogmas are rules
for safeguarding the gracious character of God's work in Israel
and Christ.[22]

To be sure, the particular form that these dogmas take is
both disputable, *and* will change with time and circumstance.
Disputes about particularity and change will vary according
to different conceptions of doctrinal development and of
language. And there lies the rub. The nineteenth-century
Roman Church was right to see that the growth of modernity
required appropriate dogmatic response. It was also right, I
believe, in taking a different path from that of Liberal
Protestantism, which was effectively, in express although not
conscious disobedience to Romans 12.2, to conform itself to
this age. But just as Liberal Protestantism tended to conform
itself to the libertarian and individualist strands of modernity,
Roman Catholicism took its cue from its equal and opposite
authoritarian and collectivist elements. The one tended to
abolish rules altogether, and so expunge the boundaries
between church and world; the other sought to extend the
rules in order to make the boundaries impermeable. Putting
the matter christologically, no doubt far too simplistically, we
might say that the one in the process lost the saving divinity of
Christ, the other the means and medium of that saving reality,
the Saviour's being like us in all things, sin apart: the divine-
human mediator of all God's dealings with his world.

III   *Dogma and the possibilities of theology*

Dogma, then, has to do with the affirmation and definition – in
the sense of bounding – of the wholeness of her vision of things
by the whole Church. Theologians, as one kind of ministers of
the gospel, have, as we have seen, a definite relation and calling
in this respect. They have a direct relation in considering

---

[22] If the Church is indeed the school of Christ, the analogy is perhaps not
unsuitable.

dogma in the light of Scripture, tradition and the whole. But they are not engaged only in the formulation and defence of dogma. They have also an indirect relation to dogma which is to be seen not so much in assessing and contributing to the articulation of confessions as in creative theological construction in their light. Here again there are clear differences of conception, which cannot be treated in detail here, on whether theology's task is chiefly or only a dogmatic one, or whether and in what sense further engagement with 'the world' is appropriate, and in what sense. But insofar as we are concerned with the relation of theologians to dogma, the following points can be made, and they return us to the opening argument of the chapter.

(1) Insofar as dogmas and confessions are properly summaries of the gospel, or aspects of it, they liberate the theologian by providing a properly delimited subject matter. One is freed by being given a rich but not infinite subject matter on which to work. The metaphor of the garden is here of relevance. There is no freedom in having responsibility to bring into shape the whole of the earth, although, of course, the gardener may draw the contents of the garden from all those plants available in the whole earth which are suitable for the soil[23] *and* thus indirectly alter the shape of the whole.

(2) This, however, works only when dogmas are truly summaries of *gospel* material: that is to say, proper specifications of the being of the God of Israel and Jesus and of his action towards and in the world. As hypothesised summaries, they are necessarily provisional – 'opinion' – having as Calvin said a relative authority over against that of Scripture. But their provisionality does not mean that they are insecure or simply at the whim of church or theologian. (We might compare here the status of an 'opinion' delivered by a judge of the High Court.) That there is theology at all – that theology has a recognisably unified body of texts, that is, a subject matter, with which to work – is due to the fact that there is a gospel which has found expression in a continuous and recognisably continuous, if too

---

[23] Compare here Barth's freedom to plunder philosophy for any concepts that happen to be suitable or adaptable for employment in the service of the gospel.

fragmented, tradition. There is, that is to say, space, but not empty space, in which to work.

(3) It is this – eschatologically founded – *space* between the gospel expressed in Scripture and the summary confessions of it which frees dogma and the dogmatics it empowers from dogmatism: the merely authoritarian and unargued assertion of merely didactic material. Only those dogmas should be affirmed which save from dogmatism. This is because dogmas populate the space between Scripture's many-sided characteris-ation of the ways of God and theology's engagement with them. If they overpopulate it, they encourage either dogmatism, by which is generally meant the merely authoritarian assertion of propositions whose relation to the gospel is not clear; or a rejection of all dogma, and along with that the gospel which it is intended to safeguard. Both those who would overpopulate and those who would deny the need for a population of any kind work with a false and over-realised eschatology, supposing either that the Church can control dogma or that she does not need it at all. Dogma, like the gospel to which it seeks to be conformed, is in the gift of him by whose Spirit alone we may anticipate with our 'opinions' the truth which we shall one day be granted to know as we are now known.

CHAPTER 2

A ROSE BY ANY OTHER NAME?

From 'Christian Doctrine' to 'Systematic Theology'[1]

I   Setting the scene

Some time during the last decade or two, courses in the University of London ceased to be called 'Christian Doctrine', and became 'Systematic Theology'. A rose by any other name? The vagaries of fashion? Or something substantive, however elusive? One way of approaching that question is to survey the influences behind the change, which were several. The addition, during the early 1970s, of a substantial Roman Catholic institution into the University had some effect, as did the frequent urging, particularly by Stephen Sykes, that the English would do well to forget the insularity that had divided them from the German tradition since some time in the nineteenth century.[2] It was also the case that for some time a shift had been taking place in theological priorities from the biblical and patristic studies that had so dominated the empirical British to a greater preoccupation with modern questions, perhaps inspired or, better, given impetus by the publication in 1963 of that celebration of popularised Bultmann, Tillich and Bonhoeffer, J. A. T. Robinson's *Honest to God*.[3] Whatever be the confluence of streams that brought about the change, it is a real one.

---

[1] First published in the *International Journal of Systematic Theology* 1 (1999), 4–23, having been commissioned for that first edition.

[2] Stephen W. Sykes, ed., *England and Germany. Studies in Theological Diplomacy* (Frankfurt: P. Lang, 1982).

[3] J. A. T. Robinson, *Honest to God* (London: SCM Press, 1963). Here a personal reminiscence will perhaps be allowed. At the time of publication, I was a third-year classics student, already being pushed towards ministry by a

But what of the substance? Is there a difference between 'Christian Doctrine' and 'Systematic Theology'? Both conceptions carry overt and hidden freights, deriving at once from their history and their usage. Christian Doctrine has the advantage of being straightforward, referring as it does to those things taught by Christians or Christianity, if there be such an entity. But there are difficulties. The title can suggest a body of teaching conveyed either authoritatively, ahistorically even, as a given and changeless totality; or critically, as a body of truth once believed but now the subject of criticism in the light of modernity's superior wisdom. (Indeed, it might be suggested that it is the waning of the star of the latter approach, increasingly revealed as jejune, that has precipitated the waxing of what has come to be called systematic theology.) In sum, the suspicion is that 'Christian Doctrine' sins against the modern canon of what is acceptable by being 'static'.

But there are complications. Increasingly popular in recent times have been courses on 'modern theology', using texts such as *Types of Modern Theology* (1937).[4] These tend to operate as comparative or developmental studies of an 'objective' kind, rather like old-fashioned courses in comparative religion, describing and classifying different approaches to modern theology, usually beginning with Schleiermacher or the Enlightenment, and moving on to the latest trends. Such courses are in general spectator courses, observing rather than participating, though to be sure containing a critical component. Yet, in their concern with such things as method, epistemology and cultural context, none of which may be prominent in Christian doctrine as traditionally taught, they give a clue to what is distinctive about systematic theology.

---

range of influences. *Honest to God* was a heady brew, putting before the reader in no doubt over-simplified form the questions raised in 'modern theology'. Yet its superficial use of Bonhoeffer's most experimental writing, assimilating it to Tillich's theology of inwardness, was recognised by some of its early reviewers. See in particular Barth's often witty remarks peppering many of his *Letters 1961–1968*, translated by J. Fangmeier and H. Stoevesandt (Edinburgh: T. & T. Clark, 1981). It was almost as if the English had discovered their Schleiermacher after one and a half centuries of sleep, even though much of the content was to be found in earlier British theology.

[4] H. R. Mackintosh, *Types of Modern Theology* (London: Fontana, 1964; first edn, 1937).

The salient fact is, however, that what we now call systematic theology emerged out of an epistemological and cultural crisis. In order to engage with that, let us broaden the historical and intellectual purview by observing that two apparently contrary features mark the history of Christian theology, almost universally. The first is that Christian thought is uniquely resistant to systematisation; and the second that the pursuit of theological truth, and sometimes of theological system, has generated over the centuries a series of outstanding intellectual talents, the equal of any other discipline or art form. Let us review something of each of them, for they are two of the keys to the answer to the question we are approaching. First, Christianity is a gospel, not a philosophy. Christian theology therefore derives from a form of divine action, mediated historically, yet involving the mysterious claim – certainly so to a certain kind of philosophical mind – that finite particulars are vehicles for the self-presentation of the eternal and infinite God. Intellectual activity involves, therefore, engagement with essentially elusive historical events, questions about which we shall encounter in our discussion of the nineteenth century.

Second, it may be asked: whence, then, comes the intellectual appeal? For Anselm, as Barth has pointed out, it is his very faith that drives him to want to understand.[5] In the relatively crisis-free atmosphere of the Middle Ages, where Bible, creed, Church and tradition were held to constitute a seamless whole, that was a relatively straightforward matter. Before and after, things are different. The intellectual side of early theology – and we shall leave on one side for now the question of whether it is properly described as systematic, or whether that epithet should be reserved for the later period – arose out of two features of the Church's life, internal ecclesiastical crisis and the Church's relation to the cultures of the world around. It is an almost universal characteristic of early Christian theology that it was prepared to accept the challenge of Jewish and Greek criticisms and objections without taking refuge in fundamentalism or sectarianism. From the beginning, Christianity was universal and missionary in scope,

---

[5] Karl Barth, *Anselm: Fides Quaerens Intellectum*, translated by I. W. Robertson (London: SCM Press, 1958), p. 18.

driven by a sense of eschatological urgency that generated a unique blend of the particular and the universal. When the urgency was to all intents and purposes lost in the Constantinian settlement, albeit recurring from time to time in Christendom in outbreaks of millennial enthusiasm, the systematic theme remained, but was, so to speak, shifted into another key. Despite all the differences that the institutionalisation of the faith brought in its train, a combination of particularity and universality remains. Just as the patristic era represents in one respect an attempt to respond to the enquiry of how the gospel of the crucified and risen Jesus had universal significance, so the Middle Ages represents in its own distinctive way the one inescapable feature of the intellectual enterprise that is Christian theology: its irrefragable relation to the culture of Greece and its artistic, philosophical and scientific successors.

Hellenism, however, was not monolithic, and all generalisations are dangerous. There are many sharp differences within the thought-world of Greece, as the example of the difference in theology between Plato and the Athenian tragedians cited by Barth has made clear.[6] And yet there are features of Greek thought that have marked the Christian conversation with culture at all times. Greece's is a theology of recollection and – although this marks more strongly its Christianisation by Augustine than it does classical Greek thought – inwardness. Recollection implies that truth is somewhere in one's past, to be sought in a quest for that which eternally is; inwardness implies that the means of the quest is already intrinsic to the inner being of the enquirer. Content, therefore, does not need to be given from without. Compared with this, we might say that the Bible's is a theology of revelation and promise, coming from without and from the future as well as the past. Does this mean that there is nothing in common between Athens and Jerusalem, as Tertullian famously asked? If there is not, what enables the conversation to take place, for conversation there indeed was and is? Part of the answer may lie in the fact that both worlds had, and have, theologies of revelation. There may

[6] Karl Barth, *Church Dogmatics*, translation edited by G. W. Bromiley and T. F. Torrance (Edinburgh: T. & T. Clark, 1957–1975), 2/2, p. 555.

be something in Heraclitus' etymological derivation of the Greek αληθες as το μη ληθον – 'true' as 'that which is not hidden' – possibly carrying suggestions of truth as unveiling, in which case there is a parallel with such biblical narratives as those in Exodus 33–34. At any rate, both cultures evidence a consciousness of divine disclosure, a common feature despite differences of mediation and content. Modern thought has tended to oppose reason to revelation, but for the world of ancient philosophy reason is the medium of divine revelation, through attention and recollection. In the ancient world, accordingly, oppositions and conversations between theology and culture operated over a far wider range of features.

The result is that the differences need to be understood within some concerns shared in common. Let us examine something of how the confluence began. Although there is a sense, to be outlined later, in which Irenaeus is a model for systematic theology, the first self-consciously systematic theology was that of Origen of Alexandria. Having outlined the beliefs of the Church, he concludes the preface to Book 1 of the *De Principiis*:

> Everyone ... who is desirous of constructing out of the foregoing a connected body of doctrine must use points like these as elementary and foundation principles ... Thus by clear and cogent arguments he will discover the truth about each particular point and so will produce, as we have said, a single body of doctrine, with the aid of such illustrations and declarations as he shall find in the holy scriptures and of such conclusions as he shall ascertain to follow logically from them when rightly understood.[7]

Origen's stress on unity and connectedness indicate what I shall call a strong conception of system, involving internal coherence and a definite logic, and it derives, as Nicholas Rescher has shown, from Aristotle. Describing this 'somewhat anachronistically' as the Euclidean model, whose 'influence and historical prominence' it is almost impossible to exaggerate, Rescher

---

[7] *Origen on First Principles*, edited by G. W. Butterworth (London: SPCK, 1936), p. 6.

shows that what has come to be called foundationalism has a long history:

> This geometric model of cognitive structure holds that the organisation of knowledge must proceed in the following manner. Certain theses are to be basic or foundational: like the axioms of geometry, they are to be used to justify other theses without themselves needing or receiving any intrasystematic justification. Apart from these fundamental postulates, however, every other thesis of the system is to receive justification of a rather definite sort. . . .
>
> On this approach . . . one would . . . construe such a system on analogy with a building whose stones are laid, tier by successive tier, upon the ultimate support of a secure foundation.[8]

Origen's foundationalism, it must be noticed, is what can be called intrinsic. The foundation stones upon which the edifice is built are the teachings of the deposit of faith, the doctrines of the creed handed down in the tradition, as they interpret biblical truth. Contrast this with the *extrinsic* foundationalism that developed with Descartes and Locke, where the foundations are from outside the system.[9] What is characteristic of Origen is his aim at a certain kind of system, logically tight after the manner of geometry, but with its own distinctive subject matter. It is this that he takes from the Greeks, not, at least not intentionally, anything of content.

Another feature shared in common with the Greeks, however varying the content given to it, is a belief, axiom indeed, that the unity of thought was in some way or other based on the unity of God or the divine order. It scarcely needs to be pointed that here the post-Kantian modern world, for all its inheritance from Greece, is a thousand miles away from the whole of the ancient world. This is also suggested by the history of the

---

[8] Nicholas Rescher, *Cognitive Systematisation A Systems-theoretic Approach to a Coherentist Theory of Knowledge* (Oxford: Blackwell, 1979), pp. 40–43.

[9] 'It is about twenty-five years ago now that I first became perplexed over the challenge so widely issued to religious people that they must have evidence for their religious beliefs – evidence consisting of other beliefs. It was insisted that at bottom a person might not *reason from* his or her religious beliefs but had to *reason to* them from other beliefs . . .' Nicholas Wolterstorff, *John Locke and the Ethics of Belief* (Cambridge: Cambridge University Press, 1996), p. x.

modern idea of system, again indicated by Rescher, that although the technical use of the term 'system' began with the Stoics' *systema mundi*, its modern usage has its origins in theology. 'By the early years of the 17th century, the philosophers had borrowed the term "system" from the theologians, using it to stand for a synoptically comprehensive and connected treatment of a philosophical discipline: logic, rhetoric, metaphysics, ethics, etc.' By the end of that century, 'System was now understood as a doctrine or teaching in its comprehensive (i.e. "systematic") development'.[10] After Kant, the stress shifts from the 'objective' system, that outside the words of the systematising mind, to the system of words itself.

But that is to get ahead of ourselves. Before moving to modern theological conceptions of system, a little more exploration of the ancient and mediaeval tradition is required. Let us return to the axiom that if God is one, truth is one. This was a truth that drove Irenaeus of Lyons, whose doctrine of God, and hence of system, was significantly different from that of Origen. The latter's doctrine of God is dominated by a concern to define God as essentially immaterial:

> God therefore must not be thought to be any kind of body ... but to be a simple intellectual existence ... Unity (*Monas*), or if I may so say Oneness (*Henas*) throughout, and the mind and fount from which originates all intellectual existence or mind.[11]

By contrast, Irenaeus' doctrine of God is dominated by a concern to establish the continuity between the God who created this material universe and the God whose Son became material within its structures. His 'system' is organised around the distinction in unity between creation and redemption, or, perhaps better, between creation, recapitulation and consummation. The intra-systematic relations with which Irenaeus is concerned are chiefly those of the economy of divine action towards and in the world, and therefore conceptual relationships take second place. It is therefore system only in a weak sense, because it is more diffident about the very possibility of

[10] Rescher, *Cognitive Systematisation*, pp. 6–7.
[11] *Origen on First Principles*, 1. 1. 6. Butterworth, p. 10.

system. Irenaeus was interested not so much in developing a system as, in Emil Brunner's characterisation, 'to perceive connections between truths, and to know which belongs to which'. Clearly, such a conception is equally committed, albeit in its own way, to general systematic criteria of coherence, universality and truth. 'No other thinker was able to weld ideas together which others allowed to slip as he was able to do ... '[12] Although, to be sure, there is a powerful conceptual dimension in Irenaeus' thought, it is secondary to a concern to articulate the coherence of God's action in the economy.

Whatever the differences between these two early theologians, mirrored as they are in myriad variations in the centuries to come – even, we might say, in the differences between Tillich and Barth – the same fundamental orientation to the unity of God and the consequent unity of truth continues to characterise the later tradition until the disturbances of the modern era. Such differences as there are derive from (1) varying conceptions of the relation between the knowability and unknowability of God; (2) differing conceptions of the nature and relation of the sources of theology, in Scripture, tradition (written and unwritten) and reason; and (3) the way in which reason as distinct from the more affective dimensions of human being – love, feeling, experience – is conceived to determine the nature of theology. As it turned out, the confluence of streams that we have already noted generated a dominating concern with the relation between the two chief sources of theology which were contributed by that twofold cultural background. Revelation was the source of what can be called passively constituted knowledge, while reason provided its corresponding active partner. If God and truth are one, nothing appears to prevent both alike from being used in the service of human knowledge. It is thus the encounter between the early theology and the philosophy of Greece which decisively shapes questions about system, for systematic thinking is above all the achievement of philosophers.

Joseph Pieper has claimed that it is to Boethius that the shape

---

[12] Emil Brunner, *The Mediator. A Study of the Central Doctrine of the Christian Faith*, translated by Olive Wyon (Philadelphia: Westminster Press, 1947), p. 262.

of mediaeval systematic thinking is owed. His principle, which was also his practice, to combine, so far as is possible, faith and reason, set the scene for scholasticism, which was an enterprise dedicated to just that. According to this account, what had to be brought into systematic relation were not the different articles of the rule of faith or creed, as Origen had attempted, but the products of two parallel but distinct sources of knowledge.[13] It was, however, an essentially religious vision, with no suggestion that philosophy was in some way 'secular', faith 'religious'. This was, as is often enough pointed out, an age of faith, and its assumption was that, because God is one, then so is truth. Described by Ingolf Dalferth as the 'Nature–Grace model' of the relationship between philosophy and theology, the enterprise, as it is represented by the greatest of the mediaevals, Thomas Aquinas, was one of co-ordination of the two sources, which are conceived to be in hierarchical relationship: 'grace is superior to nature as a source of knowledge, and faith, although inferior to reason as a mode of knowledge, is superior to it with respect to what it knows.'[14]

Yet what is interesting about Aquinas's programme as he sets it out in the first Question of the *Summa Theologiae* is how much it is in continuity with Origen's work. Alongside the pre-occupation with the relation of nature and grace, there is a similar appeal to foundations: 'just as the musician accepts on authority the principles taught him by the mathematician, so sacred science is established on principles revealed by God.'[15] There is a similar concern with systematic coherence, at least insofar as human reason is used in theology 'to argue from articles of faith to other truths'.[16] Theology is above all more a speculative than a practical science, 'because it is more concerned with divine things than human acts'.[17] In the light of its measured and lucid movement from one theme to another, one is tempted to say that if this is not systematic theology, then nothing is. If that is right, there is systematic theology in both

---

[13] Josef Pieper, *Scholasticism* (London: Faber & Faber, 1960), p. 37, citing Boethius: 'As far as you are able, combine faith with reason.'

[14] Ingolf Dalferth, *Theology and Philosophy* (Oxford: Blackwell, 1988), p. 73.

[15] Thomas Aquinas, *Summa Theologiae*, 1a. 1. 2.

[16] Aquinas, *Summa Theologiae*, 1a. 1. 8.

[17] Aquinas, *Summa Theologiae*, 1a. 1. 4.

patristic and mediaeval eras, before theology became systematically self-conscious in a different and what we call a modern way.

II   *Schleiermacher*

I introduce the next stage of our discussion by an objection arising from the essentially philosophical character of the systematic enterprise. Does this not all represent the confirmation of Harnack's famous description of the patristic enterprise as the turning of the gospel into a philosophy of religion, with its suggestion of turning theology into abstract theory? One point should be made emphatically at the outset. While there may be good reason to suspect many particular philosophical contributions to Christian theology as being contaminations of the pure milk of the gospel, it is wrong to associate philosophy as such with abstraction. I am not in this matter concerned with an opposition of theory and practice, with the suggestion sometimes entertained that what appear to be abstract conceptual concerns are in some way inimical to the bearing of a 'system' on practice. Ellen Charry has recently pointed out what she calls the aretegenic motive behind Athanasius's defence of the *homoousios*.[18] But there are many other examples. Was not Plotinus's austere and systematic exposition of the One and all that flowed from it in the interests of an equally austere ethic? For a more recent example, we have to look no further than the most relentlessly systematic theology of them all. One of Plotinus's two greatest modern successors, Baruch Spinoza, organised his system of thought around the most astonishingly rigid logic, in that everything followed from the definitions of substance, modes and the rest. It was in his own words, *more geometrico demonstrata*, demonstrated after the manner of geometry. And what was organised after the pattern of deductive Euclidean geometry? A book entitled *Ethics*. Although, like all determinist systems, this one does not finally fail to contradict itself, its ethic is none the less

---

[18] Ellen Charry, *By the Renewing of Your Minds. The Pastoral Function of Christian Doctrine* (New York: Oxford University Press, 1998), p. 97.

in the strictest possible conformity to the world-view it enunciates: a Stoic ethic of resignation corresponding to its absolute fatalism. The *systema mundi* is also a *systema humanae vitae.*

'Systems', then, are not necessarily abstract or merely theoretical; they are normally designs for living. A more justified suspicion of them is that they foreclose questions that should remain open by imposing on the material a unity that is not there. From this, as scarcely needs to be pointed, derive all suspicions of grand narratives, anything affecting to encompass the whole. To such absolute rejections, however, there are two replies. The easy one is that even the most pluralistic postmodernism does serve as a kind of grand narrative, subverting itself by pretending not to be such. Too much should not be made of this, simply because it is too easy. If there is no unity to things, then the best possible efforts should be made to show in what manner that is the case, and that is what much consciously postmodern thought seeks to do, recognising as it does the consequences of atheism. The second and real objection must be theological. The creator of the heavens and the earth is the one who confers unity on things, and systematic thinking is justified in seeking to do the best justice that can be done to this. But what kind of justice is achievable? What kind of system can be developed in parallel with or in response to the being of the creator? All depends on who we suppose God to be, how he is made known, and what are the realities and limits of our knowledge of him.

Mention of Spinoza reminds us that this mechanist philosopher became the inspiration for many a nineteenth-century thinker, activated although they often were by organic rather than mechanist metaphors. Among those inspired by the philosophy of unity, which appeared to offer so much more than the atomistic thinking of the mainstream Enlightenment, was one who can be regarded as the fountainhead of modern systematics. However, more was involved in the nineteenth-century shift from rationalism to romanticism than a move from mechanism to organism, for between Schleiermacher and his inspiration there lay the figure of Immanuel Kant, whose own development took him away from the kind of objective metaphysics of which Spinoza is but one representative, into a far more negative theology. God was real enough for Kant, but the doctrine of his unknowability was re-established in a radical form over against the theological confidence of the earlier Enlightenment. There simply was for him no direct route from either causal argument or historical fact to the God who could, nevertheless, be presumed to be around somewhere.

The only remaining route was a more indirect one than even the previous traditions of negative theology had conceived. Schleiermacher bought into Kant's ultra-negative theology, appearing to accept that the only *system* of which we can know objectively is that of nature. Because nature is a closed system, another route to theology than through its structures had to be sought, and that was the way of human experience. Now, as readers of William James will know, experience tends not to provide particularly well-defined concepts of God, because there is no particular form, apart from a myriad interpretations of subjective experience, in which he can be conceived to be present to or define himself for the knowing mind. Our language for God is subordinated to our language describing our experience of God. The outcome is that the very fuzziness of the object of thought requires a correspondingly rigid, or at least firm, systematic control if a theology is to do what is required of it – that is, to be in any sense systematic. The correlation between indefinite objects of knowledge and rigid conceptual systems is well illustrated in the thought of those figures who have in different ways influenced the shape of twentieth-century theology, the Neokantians. Deprived of Kant's confidence that there was an external world independent of the knowing subject, Cohen and Natorp placed all their eggs in the basket of an active process wherein the human mind 'objectified' or ordered its experience into a rigid systematic calculus.[19] (This conception, of course, equating as it does the objective with the objectifying, is the reason for Bultmann's refusal of any other language for God than that which is existentially mediated.)

For Schleiermacher, still in an age of relative innocence, the religious stimulations (perhaps a better translation for *Erregungen*

---

[19] Bruce L. McCormack, *Karl Barth's Critically Realistic Dialectical Theology* (Oxford: Clarendon Press, 1995), pp. 43–9.

than 'emotions')[20] give rise directly to poetic and rhetorical forms of religious language, and only secondarily and derivatively to the didactic, that concerned with descriptive instruction.[21] Dogmatic teaching therefore arises 'solely out of logically ordered reflection upon the immediate utterances of the religious (*frommen*) self-consciousness'.[22] There is therefore a hierarchy of forms, echoing Rescher's observation that, for foundationalism, 'There are two fundamentally distinct sorts of truths, the immediate and the derivative'.[23] Corresponding to the relative indefiniteness and tendency to mutual contradiction of the primary utterances is a counter-balancing stress on the systematic – meaning logically ordered – character of the dogmatic or didactic. 'The scientific (*wissenshaftliche*) value of a dogmatic proposition depends in the first place on the definiteness of the concepts which appear in it, and of their connexion with each other (*Verknüpfung*).'[24] That statement reveals a strong conception of system in terms of internal coherence, which appears to be valued above some notion of correspondence to an external reality or truth.

A number of Cartesian themes are apparent in Schleiermacher's treatment of systematic theology. Christian doctrine (*Lehre*) is only satisfactorily articulated when 'the system of doctrine has become a complete system (*Lehrgebäude*), in which every moment of the religious and Christian consciousness is given its developed dogmatic expression, and all the dogmatic propositions are brought into relation with each other'.[25] The fact that Schleiermacher uses the word *Gebäude*,[26] with its associations of building, and carrying as it does echoes of Descartes' programme of beginning the structure again on new *foundations*[27] – truly a metaphor to toy with – rather than *System*,

[20] F. D. E. Schleiermacher, *Der Christliche Glaube* (Berlin: de Gruyter, 1960), §15, translated as *The Christian Faith*, by H. R. Mackintosh and J. S. Stewart (Edinburgh: T. & T. Clark, 1928).

[21] Schleiermacher, *The Christian Faith*, §16. 1.

[22] Schleiermacher, *The Christian Faith*, §16, Postscript.

[23] Rescher, *Cognitive Systematisation*, p. 51.

[24] Schleiermacher, *The Christian Faith*, §17. 2.

[25] Schleiermacher, *The Christian Faith*, §18. 3.

[26] A word not thought conceptually significant enough to justify an entry in the *Theologische Realenzyklopädie*.

[27] The metaphor is used by the philosopher in both *Meditations*, 1 and *Discourse on the Method*, part 2. Kant was fond of the metaphor of the architectonic for intellectual systematisations.

suggests that even here, where Schleiermacher believes that he is furthest away from the hazy world of rhetoric and poetry, we are in the realm of metaphor.

This enables us to end the section with the general observation that there are many different possible meanings of the word 'system', whose original reference would seem to be to the world, or a part of it (*systema mundi*), but which has by this stage of its history come to denote the logical constructions that systematic theologies and philosophies attempt. As with all widely used and basic expressions, there is much metaphorical transfer in evidence. Here, however, we are chiefly concerned with a shift from the world to the work of the human mind. Despite this, it must be recognised that Schleiermacher's greatness as a theologian consists in the fact that, however inadequate the concept of God with which he sought to escape the pantheist overtones of his earlier writing; and despite the Kantian constriction that continued to determine much of his enterprise, he continued to be a theologian whose concern was with the reality of God. His achievement raises, as it raised at the time, the question of the nature of systems, and of what it is that they systematise. We approach that question through the work of two other nineteenth-century theologians who raise the question of system in a different form.

III   *A question of eschatology*

The famous concluding words of Stephen Hawking's *A Brief History of Time* have an eschatological ring, for to know the mind of God, in the kind of full sense implied, is something that is reserved for that time when we shall know as we are known, and even then the finite will surely not encompass the infinite.[28] It is one of the temptations of the systematic theologian to want to know more than is warranted, and what makes Schleiermacher a Christian theologian is that while he was prepared to systematise our experience, he remained diffident about anything more. Perhaps he was too diffident, for negative

---

[28] '... then we would know the mind of God', Stephen Hawking, *A Brief History of Time* (London: Bantam Press, 1988), p. 175.

theology can represent too much of a rejection of the possibility of revelation. That, at any rate, was the view of his contemporary Hegel, for whom his great contemporary's diffidence represented an evasion of the twin intellectual challenge of the tradition: of both revelation and reason. According to Hegel, Christianity was a revealed religion, revealed by the God who is essentially rational Spirit, and he used that revelation as the basis of a programme to expound divine truth as supremely rational and indeed universal truth. His positive programme, as set out in his *Lectures on the Philosophy of Religion*, is based on an unerringly perceptive critique of the rationalist reductionism or naive immediacy of the Christian theology of his time. Late Protestant attempts to ground theology in feeling or intuition, he held, fail to realise the importance of mediation. Not only does a theology of immediacy fail to account for evil;[29] it also mistakes the way by which religion arises in the human mind. Hegel is equally perceptive about the doctrinal minimalism to which this leads, reducing as it does theology's capacity, and, indeed, need, 'to know many things of different sorts, such as the ethical order and human relationships'.[30]

There is much to be said also for Hegel's envisioning of an alternative. 'The words of the Bible constitute an unsystematic account; they are Christianity as it appeared in the beginning. It is *spirit* that grasps the content, that spells it out.'[31] It seems reasonable, unexceptionable even, to hold that systematic theology is a work of the human spirit, that faculty or dimension of our being that answers to the Spirit of God. It is, however, in his construal of that spirit and of its capacities and activities that Hegel generates the errors that are so endlessly repeated in modernist theology since his time. First, as Kierkegaard was to recognise, we meet in Hegel a return to the philosophy of recollection by inwardness. 'Religion is therefore *spirit that realizes itself in consciousness.*'[32] His use of a modernised organic metaphor of the plant emerging from a seed indicates

[29] G. W. F. Hegel, *Lectures on the Philosophy of Religion. The Lectures of 1827*, edited by Peter C. Hodgson (London: University of California Press, 1988), p. 143.
[30] Hegel, *Lectures*, p. 92.
[31] Hegel, *Lectures*, p. 94.
[32] Hegel, *Lectures*, p. 104.

this clearly: 'the concept contains the entire nature of the object, and cognition is nothing but the development of the concept ...'[33] What differentiates this from classical Platonism is the injection of a measure of biblical pneumatology: 'spirit's essential [character] is *to be altogether active.*'[34] But that is not enough to take away the dominance of recollection. Second, Hegel makes much play with the need to transcend the material and finite, 'transcending all finite thoughts and finite relationships of every sort'.[35] But, as we have seen, the mediation of truth through the irreducibly finite and particular is what makes a theology Christian. Without it, one of the two contributory streams of the tradition is submerged in the other. There may be in Hegel a process of mediation, but its function is temporary, the ladder to be kicked away as higher things are attained. It owes far more to Neoplatonism than to Christianity to say, as Hegel does, that 'When human beings think of God, they elevate themselves above the sensible, the external, the singular'.[36]

Hegel's position, accordingly, avoiding as it does both a naive immediacy and a crude coherence theory of truth – for mere coherence, with no element of correspondence, cannot avoid idealism and charges of projection – provides a worthy background for the development of an opposing view. 'If I have a system, it is limited to a recognition of what Kierkegaard called the "infinite qualitative distinction" between time and eternity ...'[37] Barth's quotation of Kierkegaard's apparent rejection of system, much repeated as it is in the literature with respect to Barth's opposition to system in the *Epistle to the Romans*, can obscure the fact that in its own context it was an attack on Hegel. The latter's sin was, according to his greatest opponent, to attempt to systematise what cannot be reduced to system, and thus to falsify it. According to Kierkegaard, Hegel was in effect both reproducing a pagan identification of the human with the divine and employing a philosophy of

---

[33] Hegel, *Lectures*, p. 101.
[34] Hegel, *Lectures*, p. 102.
[35] Hegel, *Lectures*, p. 96.
[36] Hegel, *Lectures*, p. 121.
[37] Karl Barth, *The Epistle to the Romans*, translated by E. C. Hoskyns (London: Oxford University Press, 1933), Preface to the second edition, p. 10.

recollection which subverted three essential features of Christian teaching: as involving, we might say, a doctrine of creation, implied as it was in christology, which distinguished God and the world; a doctrine of revelation, not as a function of consciousness but as an implication of the need for a movement from ignorance to knowledge, given from without, if the finite was truly to know the infinite; and a doctrine of salvation, which required confession of sin and penitence as prerequisites for a knowledge of God.

At stake in the differences between these two great nineteenth-century minds is the question that still dominates theology at the end of the twentieth: what kind of articulable knowledge of God – doctrine – is possible, and how is it mediated? If that question can be answered, then so can the question of what kind of discipline is systematic theology. It has often enough been charged that while Hegel may be said to claim far too confident a knowledge of God, and that deriving from an over-confidence in human reason, Kierkegaard, with his anxiety not to transgress the infinite qualitative distinction, sins in the other direction, of appearing to make systematic theology impossible. There is much to be said in Kierkegaard's favour. He is, after all, making a protest on behalf of rationality in theology in suggesting that the philosopher may not break the law of non-contradiction, by however sophisticated a dialectical process. Moreover, 'The important point to be recognized is not whether faith is above or against reason, but that revelation is not at reason's disposal.'[38] And he is also making the traditional Christian and anti-gnostic point that a knowledge of God not both mediated by and perpetually tied to the historical Jesus Christ is not genuinely Christian knowledge of God.

Yet there remains an enduring suspicion that the Holy Spirit, if not Hegel's gnostic replacement, is not allowed by Kierkegaard to mediate the doctrinal content of the faith in such a way as to make some form of articulated teaching a genuine theological possibility. Might it be said that while Hegel too soon realises eschatology, Kierkegaard can be said to be refusing to realise it at all? Is there not, as Barth learned in

---

[38] Murray Rae, *Kierkegaard's Vision of the Incarnation* (Oxford: Clarendon Press, 1997), p. 112.

conversation with Anselm, a knowledge that still retains its character as the knowledge of faith, that remains short of sight?[39] The question of systematic theology is the question of eschatology, of how far our intellectual constructions may anticipate such eschatological perfection of knowledge as may one day be granted us. In other words, what kind of knowledge, and how far is it organisable into a whole, does the Holy Spirit grant us this side of eternity? The dispute we have reviewed suggests that one can claim for this either too little or too much.

IV   *Content and coherence*

The discussion between Hegel and Kierkegaard is important because it focuses the central question of what kind of coherence is to be sought in Christian theology. This raises in its turn the question of the object of theology. Gone, it would seem for ever, is the concept apparently underlying the mediaeval conception of theology as a matter of integrating a range of propositional claims, revealed truths, which can be derived and supported variously philosophically, theologically, or both.[40] If we are no longer concerned with verbal systematic coherence, but in some sense with the coherence of a mediated knowledge of God, then the relation of the human mind to its object must come into view. And that is the point of Kierkegaard's rejection of Hegel by means of a reassertion of the doctrine of the unknowability of God. To be sure, if God is completely unknowable, as Kant, a radical exponent of the long tradition reaching him from Pseudo-Dionysius via Aquinas, had virtually held, then we can expound, with Aquinas and his post-Kantian successors, our *language* for God rather than the self-revelation (or whatever) of God. It was that which Hegel rightly wanted to reject. Christianity is, as he repeatedly said, a revealed religion.

But how revealed, and within what limits? Kierkegaard's rightful refusal to go the Hegelian way can encourage a fear of

[39] Barth, *Anselm: Fides Quaerens Intellectum*, pp. 39–40.
[40] This seems to be the assumption of Aquinas, *Summa Theologiae* 1a. 1.

risking a proper responsibility for coherence and comprehensiveness: for Hegel's, 'to know many things of different sorts, such as the ethical order and human relationships.' Barth's treatment of the unknowability – or hiddenness, as he would say – of God as a function of revelation rather than of human ignorance may enable us to clarify this topic, however unsatisfactory may be the dialectic of revealedness and hiddenness in terms of which it is expounded.[41] God being God, there are limits, limits clearly infringed by Hegel, to what the human mind may confidently know. Yet, if God is indeed one, and if that oneness is a *revealed* oneness, thus far is there a case for ordering what we are taught of God into, if not a system, then at least a dogmatics in which (1) who and what kind of being God is and (2) the various relations between God and the world – expressed in such terms as christology, pneumatology, creation, the image of God, sin, salvation, justification, the Church, the sacraments, eschatology – are held to be related to one another. Much depends here on the relative weight given to, and the relation between, the various items. For example, a doctrine of creation will vary in relation to the weight that is given to its different christological determinants, a doctrine of atonement in relation to what is conceived to be the sickness that the incarnation, life, death, resurrection and ascension of Jesus are believed to remedy.

This in turn raises the interesting question of whether some doctrines or propositions are foundational in some sense, and consequently whether there is a hierarchy of truths, and of what kind. Here it is worth alluding to Hegel's perceptive suggestion – if that is what he is suggesting, as is not always clear with this philosopher – that not only modernist Protestantism but also Reformation attempts to read doctrine directly off the Bible lead to the kind of uninformative doctrinal minimalism about which he is complaining.[42] It is surely significant here that the magisterial Reformers were far more positive about credally and historically mediated doctrine than were some of the Anabaptists, who appeared to them to be guilty of what we might now call a romantic attempt to begin with a clean sheet. The Reformation rejected not mediation through the tradition,

---

[41] Barth, *Church Dogmatics* 2/1, for example pp. 183–4.
[42] Hegel, *Lectures*, p. 92.

but the use of the latter employed as a relatively independent *source* of doctrine.

We can scarcely begin to outline the chief points of contention here, not as the focus of inter-denominational disputes but as they illuminate the nature of systematic theology. In the work to which reference has already been made, Nicholas Rescher distinguishes between a foundation- alist conception of system, deriving, as we have seen, from Aristotle, and system as network. The 'network model sees a cognitive system as a family of inter-related theses, not necess- arily arranged in a *hierarchical* arrangement . . . but rather linked among one another by an *interlacing network* of connections.'[43] While the latter avoids the acute difficulties faced by the former, it involves, for Rescher, preferring a concept of truth as coherence to one of correspondence. The difficulties of this view, particularly for theology, are immense, and particularly of the kind presented by Feuerbach: if there is no conception of a correspondence of words to reality, what is to prevent the charge, with which we are only too familiar in this drearily reductionist age, that theological beliefs are merely projec- tions? For wherever else he was wrong about Schleiermacher, Barth was surely justified in believing that to base theology in experience was at best to give a hostage to fortune, inviting as it did the suspicion that theology was concerned *only* with experience.

If, by contrast, theology is to give reasons for saying that its systems are systems open beyond human wishes and projec- tions, then such systems as there are cannot avoid positing hierarchies, and in at least two respects. There must un- avoidably be methodological hierarchies, according to which some sources are privileged over others, and hierarchies of substance, according to which some of the contents of theology are more determinative for the nature of the whole than others. So far as the former is concerned, must it not be suggested that Scripture is prior to doctrinal tradition as a source and criterion of a theology, while the credal and ecclesiastical tradition is indispensable as a concrete focus of mediation? The reason is that Scripture both reaches us through the mediation of a

---

[43] Rescher, *Cognitive Systematisation*, p. 44.

tradition of interpretation and as the object of interpretation operates as a standard – a *canon*, as measuring rod – against which that interpretation must be measured. At the centre, as for Irenaeus and Origen alike, is the rule of faith or truth, the concentrated summary of biblical teaching. We cannot here escape, as so many theologies have attempted to do, the economic structuring of the contents of a Christian systematic theology. 'Economic' is here preferred to 'narrative' as the central way of conceiving the form of divine action under consideration, because it calls attention away from the merely verbal to the concrete, material and bodily dimensions of the biblical world. According to the rule of faith, God's action is economic in taking form in relation to the material world as a whole ('creation', 'conservation', 'providence'); in relation to specific historical events and actions (the election of Israel, the incarnation of the Word, the sending of the Holy Spirit); and in interaction with particular groups and people within that material world (Israel, her prophets, priests and kings, Jesus, the apostles, the Church, the world to whom the Church is sent). The rich plurality of divine actions and relations marks the limits to system, as well as the eschatological conditions of all human claims for knowledge. But the fact that it is an economy with which we are concerned, that of the one triune God – and because time and space structure the one created universe, we must here speak, against all postmodernism, of a version of the Aristotelian unities – makes a measure of systematic ordering both possible and necessary. This is possible because of its unity, necessary because of the form of action to which the Church is committed in its distinctive calling. Hegel's mistake was to elide some of the historical particularities which cannot be confused: Christ as human and divine, Church and world. Once again, Kierkegaard more than half sees the point: any theology whose appeal is to 'Christendom' rather than to the particular – not, however, the particular believer so much as the particular people of God – is no longer this particular form of teaching, but an abstract philosophy.

Let us look again at the question of the particular and the universal, returning first to Kierkegaard's protest in the interest of at once the gospel and the law of non-contradiction. His appeal to paradox was an appeal to logic: that when one thinks together the finite and the infinite, there are limits to what logic can do, so that language may sometimes be compelled to surface contradictions – one of the definitions of paradox? – in the interests of the inner coherence of the subject matter. 'The true artists of speech remain always conscious of the metaphorical character of language. They go on correcting and supplementing one metaphor by another, allowing their words to contradict each other and attending only to the unity and certainty of their thought.'[44] In the wrong hands, that could be a recipe for the most uncontrolled – 'postmodern' – self-indulgence, but need not be. Reality, and especially divine reality, is too elusive and mysterious for unproblematic and strongly systematic expression. We have in the interests of the particular content of Christian teaching to assert the relative validity of the law of contradiction in a weak conception of systematicity. Content must be determinative.

We approach the matter of the unity of content by asking what it is that distinguished Calvin's *Institutio* from the systems that preceded and succeeded it. Some would claim that it is not systematic theology at all, Ellen Charry citing the judgement of John Leith that 'Calvin wrote his theology to persuade, to transform human life . . .', and concludes that its themes:

> conflict with the long honoured tradition of considering Calvin a systematician. Not only do glaring inconsistencies or paradoxes suffuse the *Institutes*, but for Calvin, the truth of God is grasped as 'the personal and deeply mutual relationship of humankind to God', not as the sort of static and impersonal truth that Calvin associated with scholasticism.[45]

But that is to beg the question of the way in which Christian theology is systematic. As we have seen, one can distinguish too sharply between the intellectual and the practical. The question surely concerns the particular content of that which is treated 'systematically', and what the latter involves. One need not

---

[44] K. Vossler, cited by Michael Polanyi, *Personal Knowledge. Towards a Post-Critical Philosophy* (London: Routledge, 2nd edn 1962), p. 102.
[45] Charry, *Renewing*, p. 200, citing John H. Leith, *John Calvin's Doctrine of the Christian Life* (Louisville: Westminster/John Knox Press, 1989), p. 220.

deny the real differences between Calvin and what went before and after him. There is indeed a respect in which scholasticism was oriented to combining faith with reason, and also in which Reformed theology after Calvin was somewhat preoccupied with smoothing over the rough edges of Calvin's theology, though only a respect.[46] There is also a respect in which theology after the Enlightenment is concerned with addressing the epistemological challenge set by that movement, though by no means only that. It can readily be agreed that if preoccupations with theoretical coherence are allowed to dominate, we are better off with Christian doctrine than with systematic theology, for it is the content of the teaching that matters, albeit the teaching in harness with the other three desiderata of Acts 2.42, fellowship, breaking of bread, and prayer. (It should not be overlooked, however, that the apostles' teaching is there the first to be mentioned.)

Here we must distinguish two aspects of the systematic task. First, if it is right that theology from the very beginning has been concerned with internal and external challenges to the faith, there is more to be said than simply that Calvin – or Kierkegaard, or whoever – are not systematic theologians 'in the modern sense'. Barth may be right that the theologian's task is essentially a dogmatic one – he would no doubt put it more strongly – but it remains the case that he never ceased to read the newspaper or listen to Mozart. As he well knew, the walls of the church are permeable, so that nothing happens here without external impact, nothing happens there without implications for the way a theology takes shape. To put it another way, theology cannot engage with some of the greater nonsense coming from postmodernism into its world without paying attention to the way postmodern thought emerges out of the Christian past, and in particular out of a deficient doctrine of creation. Any concern for the truth and integrity of Christian teaching will bear upon, and have bearing upon it, dimensions of the world for whom its urgent and eschatological message is mandated, and within which the Spirit of God is never inactive.

Second, however, and this is the truth underlying the denials

---

[46] This claim will be expanded in chapter 7, below.

that theology at its best is 'systematic', is the point – and here I draw on Christoph Schwöbel's important article 'Doing Systematic Theology'[47] – that systematic theology is best understood as a particular activity done by particular people in a particular setting. The contention to which this is moving is that systematic theology owes more to the second than the first of its terms: it is theology before it is systematic, and as such the activity either of the Church or of particular members set aside for that task. These, it may be claimed, are not rightly dedicated to writing systems so much as engaging in an activity of thinking in a broadly systematic way – and that means with an appropriate measure of attention given to questions of coherence – about the content of Christian teaching, mediated as it is to them through a historical tradition. In this, general coherence may be important, but it is subordinated to an eschatologically oriented attempt to enable language to correspond to reality, God's reality.

This does not involve a naive conception of truth as correspondence. It must be such in some respect, for if the words do not in some degree correspond to the being of God and the economy of divine action in time, it is no longer Christian theology. But it is a correspondence which depends not so much on a naive view of the relation of words and the world, as on a reality *already mediated through language*. It is accordingly essential to relativise the absolute distinction we often make between words and things. 'Are not words &c parts & germinations of the Plant? ... I would endeavour to destroy the old antithesis of *Words* & *Things*, elevating, as it were, words into Things, and living Things too.'[48] The words of Scripture are neither labels pasted on to 'objective' facts out there nor, as some moderns would have it, the projections on to eternity of interpretations ('myths') by ancient minds deficient in science and philosophy.

---

[47] 'Systematic theology should not primarily be understood as a system of theological doctrines or theories, but as an activity. And since this activity is dependent on working with certain materials and using certain tools, systematic theology has the character of a craft which in some rare cases achieves the quality of an art.' Christoph Schwöbel, 'Doing Systematic Theology', *King's Theological Review* 10 (1987), 51–7, p. 51.

[48] Samuel Taylor Coleridge, *Selected Letters*, edited by H. J. Jackson (Oxford: Clarendon Press, 1987), p. 79.

Rather, they are a function of a living relationship between the creator and his elect people. The biblical books emerged out of a process of human engagement with God, as Israel and the apostolic Church lived out and lived within the historical events which were determinative for the faith. Put more abstractly: Scripture emerges through the work of the 'two hands of God', the eternal Son as the mediator of the Father's immanent engagement with the world and the Holy Spirit as the one through whom he realises and perfects that mediated interaction, in this case through the writings of the free human agents who were the authors of the canonical books.

V Systematic theology

Systematic theology takes shape in the world as the discipline concerned to engage with the reality and implications of the economy of divine action in creation, reconciliation and redemption as it is recorded in Scripture. By indwelling the biblical words and the writings of the tradition, it seeks – again, in the *koinonia* of the body of Christ and in dependence on the Spirit – both to *integrate* the various elements of the economy without depriving them of their mystery or many-sidedness and to use that economic action as the basis for a doctrine of God. The rule of faith and the various creeds can thus be understood as sedimented summaries of the economy and its implications, bearing relative but not absolute authority, in view of the fact that it may come to be realised that in particular respects they are defective in their characterisation of the biblical expression of divine being and action.[49] Theology operates within a hierarchically structured matrix provided by Scripture, the creeds, the tradition of life and thought as it is received in the present and the life of the community. It is important both because the Church communicates both to itself and to the world outside at least in large part by means of teaching and because Christianity claims to be true, in the sense of expressing the

---

[49] For example, it may appear that the threefold structuring of the creed supposes rather too modalistic an account of God's action in the world.

truth about the world and human life in its inextricable relation to God.

All thought is personal in being at once an individual and a communal process. It emerges in speech or writing from a particular mind, mediated through the physical structures of a particular body, yet as the result of a process of conversation which is at once engagement in a tradition of thought and culture, both churchly and non-churchly, and interaction with contemporaries. It is no accident that the greatest theological writing has emerged out of engagement in crises of thought and action, as the names of Irenaeus, Augustine, Luther and Barth will testify. It is not, I believe, to the advantage of the systematic theologian to be autobiographical, certainly not primarily so. The legacy of Augustine's *Confessions* is at best ambiguous. And yet it is necessary both to be clear that systematic theology, as distinct from the creeds and confessions of the churches, is characteristically the product of a single mind, or occasionally minds, and to confess that the content of this chapter owes much to conversations in student days, to begin no further back, to formative teaching and supervision, to engagement with colleagues and students, especially research students, just as much as to research, that formal activity of which we now make so much.

Systematic theology is thus an activity which is the expression of a personal skill learned in community: in a particular community, that of the Church, but that as it is set in the life of a culture still indelibly marked by its relation to the Christian faith.[50] It is, when rightly understood, dedicated to thinking in as orderly a way as possible from the Christian gospel and to the situation in which it is set, rather than in the construction of systems. That is not to say that systematically written articulations of the main features of the faith in their interrelations are a mistake. The contributions to thought that have been made by Origen, Aquinas and Tillich

---

[50] 'Boundaries between subjects ... will become permeable and as general arts courses grow more common ... it will become apparent once more what is the relation of all their components to the queen of the sciences, theology, from which, in the long history of enlightenment, they have gradually been derived.' Nicholas Boyle, *Who Are We Now? Christian Humanism and the Global Market from Hegel to Heaney* (Edinburgh: T. & T. Clark, 1998), p. 240.

are not in need of defence, even though aspects of their content, as of the content of every theology, may need to be questioned.

But that is precisely the point. The unity which systematic theology seeks, its unique way of integrating unity and diversity, is more aesthetic and moral than it is *more geometrico*. The Euclidean analogy has bewitched too many generations, and especially too many modern generations, of thinkers and theologians. The kind of unity to which a moral life or a work of art aspires has as much to do with the imagination as with the kind of disembodied rationality that has so often been the aim. The unity which imagination seeks is not, however, as is often supposed, merely projected or imposed. As the greatest poets and writers have realised, it is as much given as actively created, or rather it is a co-operation between the given and the unifying response of the mind and imagination. That is why the great works of imagination have an openness, an uncompletedness even in their perfection – a relative, rather than absolute perfection. They are the most true to the facts of the matter – 'facts' understood most broadly – when they see themselves as part of an unfinished project, that of human being in pilgrimage to its redemption. In this, theological, case 'the facts' are those we have come across in course of the argument: the history of God with his creation, its concrete expression in Scripture and other human response in worship and the life of the Church, conveyed as they are by tradition across the unbroken generations. 'For the imagination never operates in a vacuum. Its stuff is always fact of some order, somehow experienced; its product is that fact transmuted.'[51] Systematic theology, as a form of action of finite and sinful people whose achievements come as gift, generates at best anticipations of the truth that will be made known 'when Jesus Christ is revealed'; but it does indeed generate them, as its long and fruitful history continues to witness.

Does it then pretend to the right to be called 'knowledge'? That will be the subject of the next chapter.

---

[51] J. Livingston Lowes, *The Road to Xanadu* (Boston and New York: Houghton Mifflin, 1927), p. 427.

CHAPTER 3

'I KNOW THAT MY REDEEMER LIVES'

A Consideration of Christian Knowledge Claims[1]

You believe that there is only one God? Good! Even the demons believe that – and shudder. (James 2.19)

All right knowledge of God is born of obedience.[2]

I *Between gnosis and doubt*

There are a number of difficulties facing any claim that Christians know things that others do not, some of them intrinsic to the claim, others contingent on the kind of culture – whether ancient, mediaeval, modern, postmodern or whatever – in which they are made. The intrinsic ones are two. First, philosophical difficulties derive from the varying meanings and uses of the words 'to know', and their inherent complexity. As is evident from the history and variety of the discussion of what is sometimes called the problem of knowledge, we have here one of those intractable philosophical concepts which are genuinely philosophical partly because they are, at least this side of eternity, undecidable. One reason for this, it seems to me, is that there is not one problem of

---

[1] Written for the 1999 Rutherford House Edinburgh Dogmatics Conference on Truth and Tolerance, 'Christian Doctrine in a Post-Christian Society', 30 August to 2 September, 1999.

[2] John Calvin, *Institutes of the Christian Religion*, edited by J. T. McNeill, translated and indexed by F. L. Battles, Library of Christian Classics, vols. 20 and 21 (Philadelphia: Westminster Press, 1960), I. vi. 2.

knowledge, but many, because the word is used in a range of ways for which no single account can be given. This is, in turn, perhaps due to the fact that the human relation to God, other human beings and the world is so manifold that different types of knowledge claim are made in different contexts. Usage supports such an account, for it is simply not the same to know another human being well and to know the statistics of English batting performance in test matches with Australia. In terms of neither subjective experience nor objective content is it easy to identify what there is in common between such claims, although the use of the same word suggests that there is at least something. We shall examine some of the varieties of usage below when an attempt is made to summarise some biblical uses of the term.

Theologically, second, there are two chief problems. The first can be summarised under the heading of gnosticism; the second – the other side of the same phenomenon – is related to the dogma of the unknowability of God. Certain claims for knowledge are simply ruled out for Christian theology, as Irenaeus argued at length in his refutation of the heresies which have ever since been known as gnostic. Gnosticism is, simply, salvation in virtue of the possession of a knowledge, perhaps hidden from others, and involves, at the same time, a claim to a form of esoteric or superior knowledge transmitted by a secret or privileged tradition. How fine a line there is between this and what might be claimed to be justified theological knowledge is shown by the fact that forms of the doctrine of election might involve the claim that some are given to know what is, in the mystery of God's grace, hidden from others. If the polemics of the First Letter to Corinth are rightly understood to be directed at a form of proto-gnosticism, the eschatological dimensions of the matter become apparent. Paul's opponents appear to claim that, by virtue of being raised to a higher life already, they are above the usual requirements of holy living.[3] This is undoubtedly the case with Irenaeus's opponents, who claim a form of enlightenment unavailable to those who rely merely on the public teaching inherited from the tradition, and so affect a corresponding immunity from the

---

[3] I will explore this letter and this topic in chapter 5 below.

demands of the Torah. In that respect, the Reformers were effectively accusing the papacy of such an over-realised eschatology in their claims for the Church, a suspicion reinforced by later tridentine claims of an unwritten tradition known to the magisterium alone. The heart of the Irenaean counter-case to all such full and partial gnosticisms is that salvation is not by the possession of some knowledge but only by the publicly proclaimed incarnation of the eternal Son of God in Jesus of Nazareth; as we might say, in the objective content of the gospel rather than the hold of the subject upon it.

The limits of the human knowledge of God are also set by the fact that one of the attributes of God has always been his unknowability. This, however, is a doctrine whose exaggeration has had serious effects in the history of theology. The Thomist contention that we can predicate directly of God only those things that he is not can easily topple over first into Kantian arguments that God cannot be known from the world or even from revelation, and finally into post-Kantian forms of projectionism. This happens classically in Feuerbach's contention that theology is anthropology, feeding as it does Marx, Freud and other dreary modern reductionists. *Docta ignorantia* can easily lead to agnosticism. Here again the incarnation is the antidote: that if Jesus Christ is the revelation of God the Father, then a claim for revelation entails a corresponding claim for knowledge on the part of those who acknowledge it. Here we must affirm the subjective side. But that leaves open the question of the status of such knowledge, and how, on the one hand, it is to be distinguished from gnosticism, and, on the other, related to a proper doctrine of God's unknowability. This will be the subject of later discussion.

The extrinsic difficulty for those who would make claims for theological knowledge arises from the cultural dimensions of the problem, which are again revealed by 1 Corinthians. 'Jews demand signs, and Greeks seek wisdom . . .' (1 Cor. 1.22). Being loosely glossed, this might read that moderns seek certainty, postmoderns deny it, but we . . . what? Contemporary theology is inevitably bound up with the dispute of the tendencies, just as Paul clearly uses some of the language of his opponents in engaging with their false eschatology. Does not faith expect a kind of certainty – 'assurance'? As Calvin says, 'the knowledge

of faith consists in assurance rather than in comprehension'.[4]
And yet, without succumbing to the temptation to salvation by
doubt sometimes recommended by the *bien pensants* of our
discipline, how are we to avoid an over-confidence in our own
certainty? Too much may no doubt be made of the postmodern suspicion of knowledge, that it hides a will to power
and domination. And yet there is something in it. Many
Enlightenment claims to solve by reason and science the doubts
and uncertainties inherent in traditioned forms of knowledge
bear all the marks of gnosticism. Yet it is also the case that
Christian claims to knowledge have been, and frequently still
are, employed oppressively.

The point for us is that our intellectual enterprises will
inevitably be marked by the contexts in which they are carried
on. As Barth affirmed, we cannot avoid using the concepts
of the philosophers, because we operate on the same field of
contention as they.[5] Similarly, knowledge claims are implicit
even in modernist denials that we can know theologically in the
way in which we once claimed to do, or in postmodern affirma-
tions that there is no knowledge. We may be a generation that
is in danger of losing knowledge in a welter of mainly useless
information, yet to convey information is to convey that which
is claimed to be known in at least some of the multiple uses of
the word to which allusion has already been made – for
example, the times of trains or the prices in Amazon. When,
at the height of the market dogma, a senior administrator at
King's College, London, was asked by a businessman how he
justified his existence, he replied that the university made
knowledge and sold it – perhaps a prostitution of the institution
if taken as a whole account, yet undoubtedly an unavoidable
aspect. We recall here one of Justin Martyr's reasons for
conversion, that unlike the other schools of philosophy, this
one did not charge for its teaching. That was one reason for his
conclusion that Christianity is the true philosophy. Once again,
we meet our knife-edge between gnosis and doubt. Our
seminaries and especially our university departments are part of

[4] Calvin, *Institutes*, III. ii. 14.
[5] Karl Barth, 'Schicksal und Idee in der Theologie', *Theologische Fragen und Antworten* (Evangelischer Verlag AG Zollikon, 1957), pp. 54–92.

a culture dedicated to knowing, in which even those share who corner a goodly portion of the market by denying the genuineness of their own wares. What kind of a share in the culture of which we are a part is theologically justifiable, and how do we know? These are but a few of the questions which complicate our topic, little more than whose surface can be explored in one chapter.

II   *Aspects of biblical teaching*

1.   Knowledge as teaching

Aspects of the knowledge of God, can, according to the Bible, be taught. I have used in other places, so illuminating is it, Brian Haymes' account of knowledge in the Old Testament. 'Hear, O Israel: the Lord our God is one Lord. ... And these words which I command you shall be upon your heart; and you shall teach them diligently to your children ...' (Deut. 6.4, 6). Haymes comments: 'To be taught these things about God was to have knowledge of God ... It is this knowledge, rather than any particular "acquaintance experience" that is foundational for most of the people of Israel.'[6] The forms of knowledge with which we are here concerned are various, and we may instance also the knowledge as self-knowledge which is the fruit of David's experience before Nathan the prophet – the fruit of revelation through parable: 'You are the man' (2 Sam. 12.7). Similarly, the Jesus of the Synoptic Gospels demonstrates in no uncertain terms that certain things about the grace, sovereignty and law of the God of Israel are teachable beyond peradventure. Jesus also knows things, facts. John's Gospel further theologises the matter. 'Are you a teacher of Israel and yet you do not know these things?' (John 3.10). He communicates the knowledge of God, in what can only be called propositional terms. 'We speak of what we know and bear witness to what we have seen ...' (John 3.11). So also it is with the apostles' teaching, which is a teaching – 'the faith once for all delivered

[6] Brian Haymes, *The Concept of the Knowledge of God* (London: Macmillan, 1988), p. 89.

to the saints' (Jude 3) – which is to be conveyed through the ages as knowledge – knowledge of God and salvation. We can scarcely exaggerate the quantity of knowledge as teaching to be found in the pages of Scripture, and, indeed, the theological tradition which stems from it. Among the things that are claimed to be known is the knowledge of God's will (Col. 1.9) and of the revealed mystery which is the truth that Jew and Gentile are brought together in the one body (Eph. *passim*). This knowledge is presented as saving knowledge, in various forms. To know it is to know something of the source and content of salvation.

Mention has already been made of Justin's contention that Christianity is the true philosophy, and here we need to pause to consider what kind of knowledge it is that is given. It can, I think, be distinguished from many other forms of knowledge as revealed knowledge, that is to say, knowledge that is guaranteed to – rather than in – the knower because it is given by God. Thus Paul hands on what he has received, what was vouchsafed to him above all in the revelatory self-presentation of the Lord to him on the road to Damascus and in the instruction he received consequent to it. However, once committed to writing – and this is part of the continuing complexity of our situation – it is, apparently, knowledge that can be obtained simply by the reading. Or simply? Those who fail to read and learn are clearly culpable; and yet it is possible to read and fail to know, fail to recognise and understand what is there. Scripture needs to be interpreted. Although Christ is set forth in words of Isaiah, the Ethiopian does not understand – does not know – and has to be taught by one with the authority to do so (Acts 8.26–35). However objectively Scripture is the Word of God, it has yet to become such for the believer also.

We are here in the realm of knowledge by divine revelation, as the words in the story of Peter's confession demonstrate: 'flesh and blood has not revealed this to you, but my Father ...' (Matt. 16.17). John 1.18, whichever textual reading is preferred, combines a teaching of the essential unknowability of God with a definite claim for revelation: 'his only Son has made him known'. Similar important and nuanced knowledge claims are made elsewhere. Thus Ephesians speaks of knowing the love of Christ which 'surpasses knowledge' (Eph. 3.19). The control is christological, but yet involves remarkably confident claims: 'to have all the riches of assured understanding and the knowledge of God's mystery, of Christ, in whom are hid all the treasures of wisdom and knowledge' (Col. 2.2f.).

The theological pitfall is that this form of knowledge can destroy as much as it edifies. Paul's dispute with the Corinthians over their 'knowledge' that idols do not exist is particularly instructive. He concedes, in one sense, absolutely to their theology: the demons do not exist, and therefore meat offered to them is indistinguishable from meat slaughtered according to EC standards. Yet it remains the case that – quite apart from offences against love – to share in the pagan festivals risks going into the realm of the demonic in the same way as do incest and homosexual practices.[7] There is a knowledge that 'puffs up' rather than builds up, the knowledge that is the vocational temptation of those of us who do the kinds of things attempted in this chapter. Therefore perhaps we should place our forms of knowledge on a hierarchy, and acknowledge that this, though important, is not at the top of the pile.

2.   Knowledge of the heart

We are already near to the next contention, which is that for Scripture, even though God can be known by teaching, there is yet a knowledge of the heart which is generally preferred as the right human response to God. Jeremiah 31.31ff. speaks, in connection with the promised new covenant, of knowledge not from second-hand teaching but from direct personal

---

[7] It is here that something should also be said about the interrelationship of the intellectual and the ethical, because there we meet prime instances bringing out the implications of knowledge-claims for the life of the Church. We have already seen that gnosticism entails a form of knowledge-claim that takes the human agent beyond the usual demands of the law. Against this, Anthony Thiselton has recently pointed out that in 1 Corinthians, ' *"Knowledge" is inextricably bound up with respect, care and love for the other* ... If *gnosis* facilitates concern on the part of "the strong" for "the weak", *knowledge* becomes a gift (within the grammar of grace) for which Paul can give genuine thanks to God (1 Cor. 1.5b)', 'Signs of the Times: Towards a Theology for the Year 2000 as a Grammar of Grace, Truth and Eschatology in Contexts of So-Called Modernity', Presidential Address to the Society for the Study of Theology, 1999, unpublished, p. 52.

acquaintance 'they shall all know me . . .' Similar is the case with
Job's confession: 'My ears had heard of you but now my eyes
have seen you. Therefore I despise myself and repent in dust
and ashes' (Job 42.5–6). This knowledge has to be understood
as a knowledge in relation, as is classically expounded in the
Fourth Gospel. Is this gospel 'gnostic'? Not if gnosticism means
a knowledge by possession or by esoteric teaching, as distinct
from knowledge mediated by the incarnation. Central here is
John's pneumatology, which makes it clear that knowledge for
this gospel is being brought into relation with God the Father
through the mediation of Jesus Christ. The Spirit 'leads into all
truth' (John 16.13), but we are told elsewhere in the gospel
that 'the truth' is not *primarily* propositional – though we must
not forget that there are many propositions in this gospel – but
Jesus himself. To be in the kind of relation to Jesus presented
in this gospel is to know the truth. In other words what we
are concerned with here is a form of 'personal knowledge'. It
has been claimed by Professor T. F. Torrance that Polanyi's
conception of knowledge as indwelling finds its source in the
Fourth Gospel. The relation of God the Father and God the
Son in that gospel is of a mutual indwelling which is expressed
in terms of personal knowledge, rather like that which philosophers sometimes call knowledge by acquaintance. But that
gospel also makes the further point that the mutual indwelling
of the Father and the Son is extended into the finite and
human sphere in the life of the Church, and Paul's use of
expressions such as 'in Christ' surely has the same ecclesiological connotations. We might appropriately make here an
allusion to knowledge as friendship, as in Abraham's relation to
God and that promised by the Jesus of the Fourth Gospel.

This personal knowledge has two dimensions, the relational
and the eschatological. Knowledge that is mediated by the
Spirit is knowledge as gift, rather than possession, because it is
a bringing into relation with God the Father through the Son.
This kind of knowledge incorporates but marginalises the
propositional.

This knowing-that is inseparable from the knowing-of the
Father as 'the only true God and Jesus Christ whom you have
sent', which is presented here as the definition of 'eternal

life' (17.3). How could one *know* the Father who sends and
Jesus Christ who is sent without knowing *that* the Father
sends and Jesus Christ is sent?[8]

While this implies propositional claims, that is not primarily
what it entails. It is sometimes remarked of John's Gospel, and
is probably true also of Paul, that in general the noun *gnosis* or
knowledge is almost universally subordinated to verbal forms:
knowing is something that is done as the result of a relation to
God in Christ. The advantage of this is that it discourages
suggestions of the kind of possession that can lead to the
boasting of which Paul is so critical. If it is the gift of God
the Father in the Son and through the Spirit, its character as
grace and gift is less likely to be obscured. The trinitarian
matrix is brought out also in 1 Corinthians. It is not unrea-
sonable to suppose that Paul's claim in that letter that 'we have
the mind of Christ' (surely an 'apostolic' we) is not an ironical
quotation, but made positively. Those in this relationship may
confidently claim a certain kind of knowledge because God has
given it to them.

   The eschatological dimensions of this are brought out by the
often mentioned point that for Paul it is more important to be
known than to know. To be sure, to know that one is known is
a form of knowledge. But the point of putting it that way is to
maintain the eschatological limits: that the form of relation is
the condition of those who *will* know as now they *are known*,
another defence against a possible gnosticism. 'We know in
part ...' (1 Cor. 13). As everywhere in theology, eschatology
and pneumatology are inseparable. Insofar as in this sphere,
too, the Spirit acts as a down payment (the *arrhabon*, 2 Cor.
1.22) of the knowledge that is to come, the part in some way
anticipates the whole.[9] Compare 1 Corinthians 2.11: 'who
among men knows the thoughts of a man except the man's
spirit within him? In the same way, no one knows the thoughts
of God except the Spirit of God.' And Paul's purpose in saying

---

[8] Francis Watson, 'Trinity and Community in Johannine Theology',
International Journal of Systematic Theology 1 (1999), 168–84, p. 179.
   [9] Whatever that is. We should, I believe, beware of speaking of a beatific
vision – if we wish to use such language at all – in such a way as to imply that
knowledge of God will then no longer be mediated by Christ.

this is 'so that we may understand . . .' And just to complicate
the matter in preparation for the next section, it is worth noting
that the context of that final citation is a treatment not so much
of knowledge as of wisdom, another related theme which we
may not ignore. The modern world tends to equate knowledge
and wisdom, insofar as it uses the latter concept at all, but
wisdom has far more to do with the knowledge of the heart and
with the embodied and patiently tested personal knowledge
with which we are here concerned.[10] Christian knowledge is
inseparable from that wisdom that takes the form of love
exercised in community, as the whole of this correspondence
demonstrates.

III *Towards a theological synthesis*

1.   The knowledge with which we are concerned is the
knowledge of faith

As the credal or confessional nature of all our beliefs, even
those summarised in church dogmas[11] makes manifest, the
character of the knowledge with which we are concerned is
somewhere between faith and sight: it remains, as Barth showed
in conversation with Anselm, still within the realms of faith,
beyond which we cannot go.[12] Faith is a kind of personal
knowledge which by virtue of the fact that it is given – passively
constituted – remains outside the control of its recipient. It
should not therefore be understood voluntaristically – as in
some versions of the so-called Kierkegaardian 'leap of faith' –
because it is the instrument by which the human knower
is related to God the giver of knowledge. Faith is the only

---

[10] Colin Gunton, 'Christ the Wisdom of God. A Study in Divine and Human
Action', *Where Shall Wisdom be found? Wisdom in the Bible, the Church and the
Contemporary World*, edited by Stephen C. Barton (Edinburgh: T. & T. Clark,
1999), pp. 249–61.

[11] For a discussion of dogma as 'opinion', see chapter 1 above.

[12] Karl Barth, *Fides Quaerens Intellectum. Anselm's Proof of the Existence of God in
the Context of his Theological Scheme*, translated by I. W. Robertson (London: SCM
Press, 1960), p. 20. Barth seems rather uncomfortable with Anselm's view that
intellectus lies somewhere between faith and sight, but is surely right about the
eschatological limits of knowledge according to Anselm.

appropriate focus of the human knowledge of God because it is that which corresponds to the creator–creature relationship: 'Faith in God is more than the affirmation of beliefs. It is confident trust in God; it is the response of a man's whole life to God's claims; it finds its necessary expression in worship.'[13] One only has to read that citation to realise the limits of what can be claimed for this knowledge in view of human fallibility, wavering and sin. That is why faith necessarily falls short of sight. And yet it is a form of knowledge, for it is the instrument, weak and faltering as it is, of human relation to God. The translation of Hebrews 11.1 in a recent commentary brings out the instrumental and anticipatory nature of faith. 'Now faith celebrates the objective reality [of the blessings] for which we hope, the demonstration of events as yet unseen.' William Lane comments: 'The declaration ... is rhetorical and aphoristic in character. It offers not a form of definition but a recom-mendation and celebration of the faith that results in the acquisition of life.'[14] In this respect, it would be right to say that Christians are in a form of relationship, rightly characterised as knowledge, which is the gift of the eschatological Spirit, and therefore necessarily not shared by those without faith.[15]

Because, however, this is only knowledge by gift and by antici-pation, it remains subject to the limits imposed by the human condition. This is not simply a matter of human weakness and fallibility, however, but of its other pole, the unknowability of God. The God made known through the election of Israel and the incarnation is known within strict limits set by himself. The creator is known only and insofar as he interacts with the creation. That he does so in a human being indicates that he can indeed be known; that he does so, in Kierkegaard's famous description, incognito, is the other aspect which must never be

[13] *A Declaration of Faith* (London: The Congregational Union of England and Wales, 1967), p. 9. The importance of this often quoted document is that it combines avowals of belief with other forms of confession: 'We affirm ...'; 'We worship ...'
[14] William L. Lane, *Hebrews 9–13*, Word Biblical Commentary, vol. 47 (Dallas, Texas: Word books, 1991), pp. 325, 328.
[15] We sometimes speak of knowledge as saving knowledge. But how can knowledge save? It would be better it seems to me to speak here too of knowledge – and here not the intellectual knowing but personal relationship – which is the instrument of divine salvation.

neglected. The human intellect cannot and may not break through this incognito, and may not go beyond the possibilities determined by the incarnation, which therefore determines both the reality and the limits of the human knowledge of God. However much Barth's well-known dialectic of veiling and unveiling may be criticised, this much is surely to the point: that it is a christologically rather than philosophically devised doctrine of the limits of the knowledge of God. The incarnation also sets the eschatological limits, for the promise of the parousia is that there will be a universal and inescapable knowledge of God, but one still mediated christologically. To make this point is to reinforce the contention that Christian knowledge is necessarily faith-knowledge.

2.   This knowledge has an intellectual component

The limitations on knowledge are, accordingly, (1) personal – human weakness and sin; (2) theological – the unknowability of God; and (3) eschatological. We know in part and only as we are known. Yet, as we have also seen in connection with Scripture, this form of knowing necessarily includes an intellectual component.[16] As Ingolf Dalferth has remarked in connection with the doctrine of creation: 'the world is creation because and in so far as it becomes the good gift of God for us. It does not become this because we perceive it so. It does not cease to become this when we fail to perceive it so. But only when it is perceived by us in this way, is it the creation for us.'[17] Perceiving things to be what they are is part of our theological responsibility, and must be said to have two aspects. The first is a concern for the internal meaning and coherence of the things that are claimed to be known. Despite the limitations of the human mind's capacity to order the things of God within systems, expressing and ordering the truth has nearly always been seen to be part of the responsibility of the theologian. That is to say, it has always

---

[16] This personal knowledge is analogous with our knowing of other people: do I not know things about my friends that others might not, and are these not propositionally statable?

[17] Ingolf Dalferth, 'Creation: Style of the World', *International Journal of Systematic Theology* 1 (1999), 119–37, p. 137.

been believed that the truth of things can be penetrated and expounded, to a degree. T. F. Torrance has finely spoken in connection with theological rationality of 'God's revelation of himself which is not thwarted by our littleness or incapacity'.[18] Revelation is God making himself knowable, and, more than that, making the human intellect able to appropriate this knowledge. Fear of intellectual hubris should not generate a reluctance to accept responsibility for claims to know. The Christian faith has always involved an intellectual component, and the Christian Church has produced a great tradition of outstanding intellects. It may be the case that they are, along with those who exercise power in the Church, the ones in greatest danger of forms of gnosticism, but that does not invalidate the point.

The limits of the intellectual are well illustrated by the concept of heresy, one aspect of which is its premature solution of problems or of claiming to know too much too confidently. 'The Arians say, "How can that be?" as if nothing can be true unless they understand it.'[19] Similarly, Eunomianism appears to have derived much of its force from claiming too confident a knowledge of the divine essence, to penetrate to the very heart of God's inner being; and its trinitarian refutation was a refutation on the basis of revelation of the limits of human capacity to know. To know that we are known implies a propositional articulation, but woe to those who are too confident in their claim to *possess*. A characteristic modern form of this danger is an excessive confidence in the human capacity to systematise that which, by virtue of God's unknowability, is resistant to system. Despite all the provisos, however, we must not deny the implications of the incarnation, that God gives himself, in Barth's words, to 'a real human viewing and conceiving'.[20]

The second aspect of the intellectual component concerns

---

[18] T. F. Torrance, *Transformation and Convergence within the Frame of Knowledge. Explorations in the Interrelations of Scientific and Theological Enterprise* (Belfast: Christian Journals, 1984), p. 292. I owe this reference to Matthias Clausen, 'Proclamation and Communication. Apologetics After Barth?', *International Journal of Systematic Theology*, 1 (1999), 203–19, p. 206.

[19] That is a quotation, from memory, that I once heard attributed to Athanasius. Even if he did not say it, it follows from the logic of, for example, *Against the Arians* 3. 27 that it is consistent with his position.

[20] Karl Barth, *Church Dogmatics*, translation edited by G. W. Bromiley and T. F. Torrance (Edinburgh: T. & T. Clark, 1957–1975), 2/1, p. 194.

knowledge not of the internal truth and coherence of that which is revealed, but of its implications for human knowledge of the world; that is, its bearing, by virtue of its distinctive content, on matters beyond its immediate subject matter. The fact that God is made known through the mediation of his 'two hands', the Son and the Holy Spirit, has a direct bearing on our understanding of the world and human life within it. No doubt, instances of claiming for this knowledge more than can be claimed are only too common, and unnecessary conflicts with – fashionably – scientists might have been avoided with a clearer appreciation of the limits of human theological knowledge. Yet without revelation we should lack knowledge of the human condition, of the world as creation and of their overall meaning and destiny. One of the implications of revelation is, says Barth, '... to know the world as it is'.[21] The reality and limits of this are well brought out by Dalferth:

> The predicate 'created' does not refer to any perceptible difference in the world. It is not that some things are created and others not. That the world is creation may not be recognised from any particular aspect of the world, but can only be identified because it is included in the principle of the renewal of the world, its unification and perfection as creation, namely the presence of God that through actuality and possibility becomes perceptible as the good gift of God.[22]

To know that the world is created, and that God has visited and continues to visit it for its renewal and redemption is a form of knowledge available to those who will perceive what is there to be perceived.

3.   This knowledge is essentially contingent

I will first examine general features of its contingency. We have met the two crucial dimensions of Christian knowledge-in-relation already: that because salvation is by the incarnation,

---

[21] Barth, *Church Dogmatics*, 4/3, p. 769.
[22] Dalferth, 'Creation', 137.

any other focus ceases to be the knowledge of faith; and because the giver of our knowledge of that salvation is the Holy Spirit, any other conception than that which is passively constituted is excluded. Let us explore the first as it impinges on the nature of the act of knowing. What does it mean that knowledge is dependent upon the incarnation? It means that it is mediated through an event that is contingent, and therefore over Lessing's now almost mythical ugly broad ditch. Lessing's challenge, we must remember, was welcomed by Kierkegaard because it highlighted both the gnostic enormity of Hegel's attempt to know the workings of the divine *Geist*, and the corresponding necessity that the knowledge of salvation was mediated only through the needle's eye of the incarnation and cross.[23] We, finite and fallen human beings, know only contingencies, and only through contingencies – indeed, in this case, a contingency which offends both intellect and moral sense. There is nothing else.

One of the blessings of some recent epistemology, not at its postmodern extremes so much as in its stress on fallibilism, is that it becomes easier – easier, but not thereby easy – to defend the doctrine that all human knowledge is finite and fallible, without being any the less describable as knowledge. As some commentators on the recent A-level results have shown, when standards are reduced, more are caught in the net. And it is undoubtedly the case that modernist theories of knowledge tended to over-stress both human capacity and the privileges of certain forms of knowledge, mathematics and science, for example, in consequence setting impossibly high standards for what might count as knowledge. That the over-realised eschatology of the Enlightenment is now in retreat can only be the source of encouragement, for it means that all human knowing is more like that which theology has always proclaimed if not always practised, that theology is *theologia viatorum*, the theology of those who have not yet arrived at their destination. As we have seen, the knowledge of faith is the knowledge given to those who are human persons: that is to say, embodied, finite

---

[23] Søren Kierkegaard, *Concluding Unscientific Postscript*, edited and translated by Howard V. Hong and Edna H. Hong (Princeton: Princeton University Press, 1992), Book Two, Part One, entitled 'Something about Lessing', begins with 'An Expression of Gratitude'.

in time and space. Richard Holmes refers to Coleridge's view that 'certain kinds of knowledge can only be gained by a slow transitional passage through mystery and doubt, as opposed to a rapid logical unfolding ...' And he cites him: 'For how can we gather strength but by exercise? How can a truth, new to us, be made our own without examination and self-questioning ... But whatever demands effort, requires time ...'[24] This in turn enables us to say a little more about what is meant by the knowledge of the heart, that it is not intellectual (rationalism) nor experiential (pietism, Schleiermacher) but of the whole embodied person, compact of intellect, will, emotion and imagination, to name but a few of what can cautiously be called our faculties, in the sense of different ways of construing the human relation to that which it affects or wishes to know. We here meet again the way in which this knowledge can be construed as a form of God-given wisdom, something to be progressively but, as they say, asymptotically appropriated and lived in during the human pilgrimage. So far, accordingly, as the knowledge content of this human condition is concerned, Michael Polanyi's characterisation not just of religious knowing but of the whole human intellectual enterprise is worth quoting again: 'that I may hold firmly to what I believe to be true, even though I know that it may conceivably be false.'[25]

4.   The contingently mediated form of knowledge with which we are concerned is also in its own way unique

Christian knowing, although from the point of view of the knower simply another form of human relation to reality, is, as we have seen, by virtue of its content, also distinctive.

> Theology is ... 'metaphysics'. That is, it claims to know elements of reality that are not directly available to the empirical sciences or their predecessor modes of cognition,

---

[24] Richard Holmes, *Coleridge. Darker Reflections* (London: HarperCollins, 1998), p. 205, and citing Samuel Taylor Coleridge, footnote to the 1812 edition, in *The Friend*, II, p. 81.
[25] Michael Polanyi, *Personal Knowledge. Towards a Post-Critical Philosophy* (London: Routledge, 2nd edn 1962), p. 214.

but that yet must be known – if only subliminally – if such lower level cognitive enterprises are to flourish ... [T]heology claims to know the one God of all and so to know the decisive fact about all things, so that theology must be either a universal and founding discipline or a delusion.[26]

The incarnation is not just another event, not just another object of human enquiry. It is the unique event in which the eternal Son of God became incarnate through the Holy Spirit in the womb of the virgin Mary. Therefore, we cannot escape, either, the fact that just as this was brought about by the Spirit, so it can only be known by the same agency. This is another way of saying that faith is the gift of God the Spirit: to be obtained not by human will nor by historical research, but by the gift of God. One point of this is that, just as the Spirit calls attention away from himself to the one who is the Truth, so this way of knowing calls attention away from the mechanics of the knowing to that which is known by being confessed.

5.   This has also an ecclesial dimension

It is not so much Christians who know, as the Church. Creeds and confessions more often than not are expressed in the first person plural: 'We believe ...' Individual believers know even more 'in part' than the community of faith, which to that extent represents them in the world and before God. Now, this may seem to be a rather idealistic picture, and indeed in certain respects it is. The Church's knowing has its limitations and fallibilities also. The Council of Chalcedon divided as well as united those separated by christological differences, so that even at the time its achievement was ambiguous. But it remains the case that despite the treason of the theologians which so marks our era, church bodies have for the most part maintained the apostolic teaching, and that what individuals find difficulty in accepting, where individuals falter and doubt – because we are but individuals – the Church, as a community

---

[26] Robert W. Jenson, *Systematic Theology* vol. 1, *The Triune God* (New York and Oxford: Oxford University Press, 1997), p. 20.

over time and space, confesses more or less confidently and unitedly.[27] Robert Jenson quotes Maximus the Confessor:

> 'The one who knows the mysteries of the cross and the tomb, knows the reasons of things. The one who is initiated into the infinite power of the Resurrection, knows the purpose for which God knowingly created all.'

Maximus' knowledge is that of *initiates*, into a mystery event. Those who are baptized into Christ's death and say 'Amen' to the Eucharist's prayers and behold the fraction of the bread that is Christ's body, these are the ones who know the goodness of the creation ... The great 'nevertheless' cannot finally be resolved from the conceptual outside; but it can be liturgically inhabited.[28]

However, this – what might be called the cultic dimension of the matter – requires supplementing by a recurrence to the notion of personal knowledge, in order to bring out its broader participatory aspects. Being 'in Christ' involves a form of personal knowledge of God realised by participation in the worship and life of the Church.[29] There is therefore a dynamic to the process,[30] which means that this knowledge cannot be reduced to propositional form. It generates true propositions, perhaps even some timelessly true ones – 'God is love' – but the knowledge of which we speak is the knowledge of those placed in the life of a community centred on and ordered around one whose presence-in-absence[31] implies a certain status for the knowledge. It is the knowledge of those for whom final certainty is not yet a possibility, anticipations of which may yet

[27] Here we must freely confess that although the Reformers were far from being individualists, many forms of more recent Protestantism, pietist and rationalist alike, have contributed to the loss of the churchly dimension of our standing before God. Further, the point being made here is not intended to concede to the tendency to treat the clergy as substitute believers.

[28] Robert W. Jenson, *Systematic Theology*, vol. 2, *The Works of God* (New York and Oxford: Oxford University Press, 1999), p. 24.

[29] It is in this respect, as Trevor Hart pointed out at the first delivery of this piece, that knowledge by acquaintance need not be considered individualistically.

[30] As Brian Brock pointed out during the discussion of the paper.

[31] See Douglas Farrow, *Ascension and Ecclesia. On the Significance of the Doctrine of the Ascension for Ecclesiology and Christian Cosmology* (Edinburgh: T. & T. Clark, 1999).

be granted by the Spirit in ways corresponding to the many dimensions of our human being, intellectual, aesthetic and moral alike.

IV *Uncomfortable conclusion*

That the creeds and confessions of Christendom contain reference to the Church entails that those who accept the gospel message submit at least part of their judgement to an authoritative teaching which is mediated by an institution and a tradition (or traditions). Calvin is surely right to say that we do not believe *in* the Church as we believe *in* God; it is preferable to say that we 'believe the Church'.[32] And yet even in that form there are contained two offences against the spirit of the age, against political correctness even. Modern individualism is offended that individuals should submit themselves to the dogmas of an institution, with the possible – and highly significant – exception of the State; while the ideology of tolerance is offended by the categorical claims for truth which the gospel makes. Much modern tolerance is, to be sure, little more than a means of the repression of uncomfortable opinion, encapsulated in forms of political correctness and illustrated by the experience of a colleague who was once told: 'You can't say that; we are tolerant here.' What needs to be reiterated is that all positions, including relativism, are positions, and thus far exclusive and intolerant of those positions which are logically incompatible with them;[33] and all ideologies and theologies take some institutional or communal form. Christian exclusivism, insofar as it maintains an awareness of the eschatological limits of its own knowledge claims – and the historical weakness of its position is that it has not always done so – is, or ought to be, able to maintain a due balance of tolerance and intolerance.

The stress of this chapter has been on knowledge mediated by the incarnation, which itself represents a kind of relentless

---

[32] Calvin, *Institutes*, IV. i. 2.
[33] This is well illustrated in Gavin D'Costa's critique of the concept of religious pluralism. 'The Impossibility of a Pluralist View of Religion', *Religious Studies* 32 (1996), 223–32.

intolerance: a refusal to tolerate the rule of sin and evil. The value of such passages as Jesus' expression of invective against certain forms of religiosity – 'woe to you, scribes and Pharisees, hypocrites!', uttered five times in Matt. 23 – is to show that he was not a tolerant man. And yet the means of its expression was from beginning to end unrepressive, even to the cross. That may be part of the cost the Church will pay for following that lead in the repressive postmodern world. But it also leads us to the question for the next three chapters. The personal, relational and dynamic character of the knowledge with which we are concerned has been expounded. What bearing might this have on the question of action, of ethics? We begin with a discussion of the relation of systematic and moral theology.

CHAPTER 4

A SYSTEMATIC TRIANGLE

Hegel, Kierkegaard, Barth and the Question of Ethics[1]

I *Systematic theology again. An old theme in a new context*

Why are people often so suspicious of systematic theology? A number of reasons might be given, among them the anti-intellectualism which is too apparent in parts of the churches, though one hopes, not entirely confidently, is absent from the universities. To be taken more seriously are the various forms of reproach against the premature systematisation of that which cannot be systematised. They take two forms, first the negative, which has, I suspect, a source in certain forms of negative theology – 'we can say of God only what he is not' – and runs the risk of a retreat from the biblical narrative either to forms of abstraction or to post-Kantian projectionism. If, that is to say, there is no concrete knowledge of God as he is, then systematic theology will take the form of an abstraction of some kind from God's effects (as in some forms of Thomism) or of the systematisation of the supposed implications of experience. The second reproach against systematic theology finds its basis in an assertion of the resistance of the biblical revelation to systematisation by virtue of the character of the 'positive' knowledge that is claimed to be given. A 'Kierkegaardian' objection to systematic theology would begin here, but we must be aware at the outset that his is a positive theological stance, based, so to

---

[1] Written for a conference of the Research Institute in Systematic Theology, King's College, London, on the theological significance of Søren Kierkegaard, March 1999.

speak, on revelation: on an apprehension of the kind of deity made known in Scripture.

We can begin to explore the nature of the question with another reference to the account of what he is doing by the first self-consciously systematic theologian of the tradition, Origen of Alexandria. As we saw in chapter 2, for Origen Christian theology involves an attempt to produce 'a single body of doctrine' by the systematic development of interconnected teaching on the basis of first principles. Those first principles, the foundation stones upon which the edifice is built, are the teachings of the deposit of faith, the doctrines of the creed handed down in the tradition, as they encapsulate biblical truth. The justification, let us not forget, is theological: the oneness of God supports the oneness of the human intellectual construction.

The chief danger here is not of a theology bypassing revelation, but of too confidently claiming to achieve system on its basis. We might say that this is the danger of what is called scholasticism, in the pejorative sense sometimes attributed to the two main movements so described, mediaeval scholasticism and the Protestant scholasticism of the centuries after the Reformation. Without wishing to caricature these two movements, it is possible to hold that in certain respects they exceed limits which ought not to be exceeded. Their perennial temptation is to concentrate on the verbal systematisation of the content of the faith at the expense of – what? A character-istic reproach against the two traditions is that they favour the reorganisation of given teaching rather than deeper penetration into the subject matter. So, Werner Elert accused the theologians after the end of the patristic era of simply working within the conceptual framework provided by Chalcedon without seeking further penetration into its mysteries: reorganising concepts rather than exploring that to which they make reference.[2] The charges against Protestant, and particularly Reformed, scholasticism are similar, and twofold. That much weary debate about relatively peripheral doctrines like predestination distorted the overall teaching of

---

[2] Werner Elert, *Der Ausgang der altkirchlichen Christologie* (Berlin: Lutherisches Verlagshaus, 1957), pp. 10f., 22, 64, 235.

the faith; and that there developed a stress on the merely verbal orthodoxy of expression which favoured an intellectualistic understanding of faith as consisting in the formal articulation of things believed, of a creed. Here suspicions of systematics derive from the claim, whether right or wrong, that systematisation generally militates against depth and balance because it does not do justice to that which lies beyond the verbal recital of *credenda*. It generates, that is to say, a false immediacy: a claim to know God when one knows the right formulations.

Insofar as the deficiencies of both mediaeval and Protestant scholasticism derive from an over-confidence in possessing the truth of doctrine, they represent a marked difference from that of most modern forms of systematisation, which tend to the opposite: to a projectionism which serves to compensate for the denial of the possibility of realistically construed doctrine. The negative theology of Immanuel Kant generates an agnosticism about the objective world and a compensating reliance on the projection of creative mind, spawning as it does ultimately the worlds of Kaufman and Cupitt. Even though Schleiermacher cannot be held responsible for their excesses, he does appear to concede too much to the Kantian metaphysic of mind. That, at any rate, was the view of his contemporary Hegel, for whom his great contemporary's ontological diffidence represented an evasion of the twin intellectual challenge of the tradition: of both revelation and reason. According to Hegel, Christianity was a revealed religion, revealed by the God who is essentially rational Spirit, and he used that revelation as the basis of a programme to expound divine truth as supremely rational and indeed universal. His positive programme, as set out in his *Lectures on the Philosophy of Religion,* is based on an unerringly perceptive critique of the rationalist reductionism or naive immediacy of the Christian theology of his time.

Because there is already in chapter 2 a comparison of Hegel and Kierkegaard, I shall here merely summarise the main points as an introduction to the three-point comparison which will focus the enquiry. In favour of Hegel are the following features of his thought. First, he is aware of the necessity of historically mediated articulations of doctrine. For him, any evasion of mediation evades also the problem of evil and can account neither for human theological thought nor for the richness of the sets of relationships with which theology has to do.[3] Second, Hegel realises that the theological interpretation of Scripture is a pneumatological matter, when the human spirit in some way responds to the action of the divine.[4] Third, his use of a modernised organic metaphor of the plant emerging from a seed differentiates his position from classical Platonism and represents the injection of a measure of biblical pneumatology: 'spirit's essential [character] is *to be altogether active*'.[5] But the faults are the mirror images of the virtues. It is in his construal of the spirit and of its capacities and activities that Hegel generates the errors of Promethean heaven-storming that have been so endlessly repeated in modernist theology since his time.[6] Too much is attributed to the intrinsic capacities of the human mind, and it was against the background of some of the outworking of Hegel's immanentism that Barth famously reasserted a Kierkegaardian position early in his career.[7] Hegel's sin was, according to Kierkegaard, to attempt to systematise what cannot be reduced to system, and thus to falsify it. According to him, Hegel was in effect both reproducing a pagan identification of the human with the divine and employing a philosophy of recollection which subverted essential features of Christian teaching. The critic of immediacy is himself caught in the act of, we might say, appearing in public unclothed.

Thus there are points to be made on both sides, and it is here that reference to Barth enables a measure of arbitration. It has often enough been said that while Hegel may be said to claim far too confident a knowledge of God, Kierkegaard, with his anxiety not to transgress the infinite qualitative distinction, sins

---

[3] G. W. F. Hegel, *Lectures on the Philosophy of Religion. The Lectures of 1827*, edited by Peter C. Hodgson (London: University of California Press, 1988), pp. 143, 92.

[4] 'The words of the Bible constitute an unsystematic account; they are Christianity as it appeared in the beginning. It is *spirit* that grasps the content, that spells it out.' Hegel, *Lectures*, p. 94.

[5] Hegel, *Lectures*, p. 102.

[6] 'Religion is therefore *spirit that realizes itself in consciousness.*' Hegel, *Lectures*, p. 104.

[7] 'If I have a system, it is limited to a recognition of what Kierkegaard called the "infinite qualitative distinction" between time and eternity ...' Karl Barth, *The Epistle to the Romans*, translated by E. C. Hoskyns (Oxford: Oxford University Press, 1933), Preface to the second edition, p. 10.

in the other direction, of appearing to make systematic theology impossible. Might it not be said that while Hegel too soon realises eschatology, Kierkegaard can be suspected of refusing to realise it at all? The question of systematic theology is the question of both mediation and of eschatology, of how far our intellectual constructions may anticipate such eschatological perfection of the knowledge of God that may one day be granted us. In other words, what kind of knowledge, and how far is it organisable into a whole, does the Holy Spirit grant us this side of eternity?

II *Two accounts of theological ethics*

I shall approach the question by a discussion of aspects of ethics in the three theologians. The value of ethics is to be found in focusing questions in different ways from a more purely doctrinal discussion. Ethics – unless that discipline is conceived merely rationalistically as the articulation of timeless maxims of behaviour – brings into sharp focus the relation between divine and human action. To be sure, so does christology, so that I must pause to be more precise. As the work of the scholastics, both mediaeval and Protestant, shows, it is possible to make a fairly neat systematic organisation of those things that are believed and taught about Christ, with the help of concepts refined over the tradition. God, the incarnation, the person and work of Christ and his continuing work as prophet, priest and king, can be brought into systematic order in such a way that their relation to each other and to other theological loci can be laid out in a faithful, orderly and lucid way. The danger, as we have seen, is an excessive zeal for coherence, resulting in what Barth tended to regard as the abstractness of formulae like that of Chalcedon. But that is not the chief point here, which is that however well and humbly this is done, it primarily concerns the spelling out of the implications of one historical person, and, indeed, one who has generated over the centuries a set of continually refined concepts. Ethics is concerned with the relation of God to human action in an even less manageable context than the christological.

Again I must be careful. It is not the case that there has been no similar tradition of careful thought and conceptual development in the field of theological ethics. In its own way the tradition is as rich and many sided as that of christology. The difference is that, except on certain rationalistic premises, there is an openness and indefiniteness here which goes beyond that allowed by the once-for-all incarnation of the Word. We are concerned with the immense variety and richness of the human, in this case specifically Christian, response to the gospel in all the variety of the social forms in which the Christian life has worked itself out. Is it partly the case that when christology gives way to pneumatology, as to some extent it must, things become, because more definite and particular, less subject to generalisation? Here two points should be made. The first is that every act of the Spirit enabling the world to anticipate its perfection is particular, and therefore to be subjected to general concepts only with fear and trembling. The second is a counterbalancing claim, that because the Holy Spirit is the Spirit of truth, as in dogmatics proper, so here, ethical truth is meant to be uttered, and that means intelligible truth.

In this light, let us look at our subjects. First, Kierkegaard. The charge against Kierkegaard, as famously expressed in Ibsen's *Brand,* is that on his premisses, it is impossible to distinguish between the saint and the madman.[8] Is it enough to distinguish Abraham's intended act from murder by attributing it to divine command? If we are to answer the charge we must first bear in mind that Kierkegaard's work in *Fear and Trembling* is not a treatise on moral theology so much as an exploration of limits. There is to be discerned operating in this work a particular conception of divine and human action, as represented in the relation between God and Abraham. Its focus is upon faith as a mode of human being before God, and this involves the kind of trust that, as Paul saw, is essential to being a Christian: 'for it is great to give up one's desire, but it is greater to hold fast to it after having given it up; it is great to lay hold of the eternal, but it is greater to hold fast to the temporal after having given it up.'[9]

---

[8] Stewart R. Sutherland, 'Saintliness and Sanity'. A Public Lecture delivered at the University of Stirling, Scotland, 1979.

[9] Søren Kierkegaard, *Fear and Trembling,* edited and translated by Howard V. Hong and Edna H. Hong (Princeton: Princeton University Press, 1983), p. 18.

There is, surely, an implicit confidence in divine providence operating somewhere in the background. And there is another important respect in which we are presented in this great text with an authentically biblical God. As Walter Moberly has recently written, Genesis 22 is part of a great tradition of writings in which God is presented as subjecting his faithful to testing, almost to their limits. As he does not fail to conclude, Jesus is the definitive instance of those so tested, in his case up to the very limit of human endurance of God-forsakenness. In that respect, the objections of the moralists, right up to and including the absurd recent charges of 'divine child abuse', simply cannot be taken seriously.

Another way in which we must be sure to read Kierkegaard is as an answer to the ethical self-confidence represented by Hegel. Kierkegaard's concern is to maintain the proper distinction between the creator and the creature. If God is the creator, then certain corollaries follow. One is that human beings cannot and may not realise themselves except as creatures, and that means as those who are dependent. Another is that the ethical agent cannot be justified apart from redemption, and it is surely right that *Fear and Trembling* appears in at least one of its translations alongside *The Sickness unto Death.* For our purposes, the point is this: we are not given, and not to expect, from Kierkegaard a *theory* of divine–human relationship, and certainly not a theory of ethics. Despite this, however, it could still be the case that the theologian can expect or request more. Might not the Holy Spirit be requested to guide into all truth in the ethical sphere also? Might it not be possible to render something more of an account of the relation of the believer to God as a means to understanding how the response takes shape as a function of obedience to divine command? In sum, what *kind* of reasons is theology expected to give in support of its positions?

It is, theologically, right to read Hegel's proposal as a proper attempt to answer such questions. Hegel may not be, and, if Kierkegaard is right, certainly is not, a model Christian thinker, but he is nonetheless to be taken as a theologically and morally serious thinker. He is also, in one respect, responding to the same realities as his Danish opponent. With the death of Christendom – we might say, with the loss of the scholastic way of encompassing the systematic certainties of the Christian world-view – there is a real intellectual and ethical crisis for the world that was once Christendom. That Hegel plans a restored Christendom on the basis of a possibly pagan theology is not here to the point. What is is that the moral breakdown that he so well discerned has progressed beyond all measure since his prophecy, and that we should take seriously his view that modernity is a theological crisis, a crisis of the human relation to God. His achievement in ethical thought is to see that the response of early modernity suffers from what he calls abstractness: a failure to root moral theory in the way in which human beings relate to one another in society. Even Kant, for all his social and political concern, is finally individualistic. Against this, Hegel's proposal was to renew that relation by an audacious – systematic-theological? – philosophy in which the human relation to God was at the centre. There are strengths to this, too. Barth has rightly pointed out that one of the weaknesses of Kierkegaard's theology is its lack of an ecclesiology.[10] Hegel has one, even though, by taking the world to be the Church, he may be thought to fail to diagnose the real disease. Nevertheless, if we lay on one side the connotations that the idea of the State has gained in this century – the repressive or nannying, self-divinised, bureaucratic Leviathan of recent times – we shall find that it is worth pausing for a moment over what Hegel says.

> The state is the actuality of the ethical Idea. It is ethical mind *qua* the substantial will manifest and revealed to itself, knowing and thinking itself, accomplishing what it knows and in so far as it knows it ... [S]elf-consciousness in virtue of its sentiment towards the state finds in the state, as its essence and the end and product of its activity, its substantive freedom.[11]

It is not too much of an oversimplification to say that Hegel's problem with both Hobbesian and the apparently more genial

[10] Karl Barth, 'A Thank-You and a Bow – Kierkegaard's Reveille', *Fragments Grave and Gay*, translated by Eric Mosbacher (London: Collins, 1971), pp. 95–101, p. 99.

[11] *Hegel's Philosophy of Right*, translated by T. M. Knox (London: Oxford University Press, 1952), §257, p. 155.

theories of liberalism is that they fail to allow that freedom is to be found in relation to others. Freedom comes in realising our reality, which as intellectual mediators of the divine idea we can embody only in social institutions.

Secular interpreters of Hegel see this point: 'Personhood and subjectivity can be actualized only by being given concrete embodiment in the roles of a harmonious social system or ethical life.'[12] What they are less comfortable with acknowledging is its trinitarian basis, for it is in self-consciousness that according to Hegel we realise our relation to universal *Geist*, who – or which – does bear some kinship with the third person of the Trinity. In this respect, Hegel is a recognisably Western, indeed Augustinian, theologian. For has not much Western theology understood the Spirit as a form of God's immanence, within the Church or within the individual or, in this case, within the mysterious developments of human culture? Kierkegaard's protest in the name of divine transcendence against this effective self-divinisation of the human is fully justified. Yet once the pneumatological cat has been let out of the bag, it remains to tantalise us. If pneumatology is a function of the inner and immanent, there are certain features of the Spirit's relation to the world, prominent in Scripture, which fail to come to expression.

III   *And so to Barth*

Let us approach the problem of pneumatology through a review of aspects of Barth's ethics as John Webster has recently expounded them so illuminatingly. Let me lay the cards – or at least some of them – on the table at the outset. There is a lesson to be learned from the great Hegel, who oriented himself to the third person of the Trinity, albeit one scarcely identifiable with the self-effacing and transcendent person of Scripture. We can grant the two major and decisive weaknesses in Hegel's theology. His Prometheanism, like that of much of the modern

---

[12] Allen W. Wood, 'Hegel's Ethics', *The Cambridge Companion to Hegel*, edited by Frederick C. Beiser (Cambridge: Cambridge University Press, 1993), pp. 211–33, p. 218.

world, derives first from pneumatological immanentism – a tendency to *identify* the Spirit with the human agent – and second from an over-realised eschatology memorably indicated by Barth's dictum that 'Hegel's living God – he saw God's aliveness well, and saw it better than many theologians – is actually the living man.'[13] Yet it can nevertheless be asked whether a Spirit more transcendentally conceived and less realised might assist in developing a theology of mediation more ecclesially formed than Barth's.

Professor Webster indicates in one italicised observation the continuity between Hegel and Barth (though without making this his point): '*[F]rom the very beginning, Barth's theme is God and humanity as agents in relation.*'[14] This involves an account of the relation of God and the human agent containing rather more detail than we gain at least from the Kierkegaard of *Fear and Trembling*. It requires what he calls a 'moral ontology'.

> In so far as it is a 'moral ontology', therefore, Barth's dogmatics can be construed as an extended enquiry into the moral field – into the space within which moral agents act, and into the shape of their action, a shape given above all by the fact that their acts take place in the history of the encounter between God as prime agent and themselves as those called to act in correspondence to the grace of God.[15]

As we know well, Barth's is essentially a theology of grace, and specifically that covenantal grace which is grounded in the inner-trinitarian, electing, love between the Father and the Son. But the election that takes historical form in Jesus Christ is election to something, to a form of obedience, and hence the structure of *Church Dogmatics* 2/2, with its ethical section flowing out of the theology of election. This means, in Webster's words, that, 'Grace is imperatival. And ... the imperatival character of grace, its character as command, is emphasised in order to confirm the place of the human agent in response to grace'.[16]

---

[13] Karl Barth, *Protestant Theology in the Nineteenth Century: Its Background and History*, translated by B. Cozens and J. Bowden (London: SCM Press, 1972), p. 419.

[14] John B. Webster, *Barth's Ethics of Reconciliation* (Cambridge: Cambridge University Press, 1995), p. 33. Italics are in the original.

[15] Webster, *Barth's Ethics*, p. 4.

[16] Webster, *Barth's Ethics*, p. 51.

As in Hegel, there is a concern with the establishment of freedom: 'God's claim which, as *permission* is "the granting of a very definite freedom".'[17]

What this and the subsequent study of Barth's ethics make clear is that Barth is concerned with the way in which divine action establishes – and that means enables but does not compel – right human action. But one revealing feature is apparent in the light of Hegel's ethic: that the treatment, in tending to be concerned with the relation between divine action and the human being individually conceived, may be in danger of the dread charge of abstraction. That is not to say that Barth has an individualistic anthropology. If we examine his cumulative definition of human beings, as those who give and receive assistance gladly to and from one another, we shall find a relational view of the human rooted in a prior triune relationality – effectively, indeed, a Trinity more relationally conceived than the threefold 'I' of the earlier work.[18] What I do not see much evidence for is a bringing of the two – the relational anthropology and the theology of ethical action – together into some kind of harness. What, we might ask here, is the principle of formation in Barth's ethics? The answer is to be found in christology and a conception of grace.

Barth's model for the ethical relationship with God is, rightly, christological. It appears in so many places that I can perhaps be forgiven for summarising it. First, the inner-trinitarian relation between the Father and the Son is a relationship of command and obedience. Command and obedience are written into the structure of divinity, so that it is as godlike to obey as it is to command.[19] This relationship, second, takes historical form in the relation between Jesus and his Father, so that in Barth's memorable treatment ethics is based in the command of God in whom we may believe because he comes alongside us and humanly provides the only proper basis for free obedience.[20] There is, I think, as always an analogy at work:

[17] Webster, *Barth's Ethics*, p. 55, citing Barth, *Church Dogmatics*, 2/2, p. 585.

[18] Karl Barth, *Church Dogmatics*, translation edited by G. W. Bromiley and T. F. Torrance (Edinburgh: T. & T. Clark, 1957–1975), 3/2, §45. 2, pp. 222–85.

[19] On this, see Eberhard Jüngel, *Gottes Sein ist im Werden* (Tübingen: J. C. B. Mohr (Paul Siebeck), 2nd edn, 1967), p. 100.

[20] Barth, *Church Dogmatics* 2/2, pp. 556–65.

the relation between God and Jesus Christ becomes an analogy for that between God and ourselves. Here, as in all Barth's theology, there is an analogy of grace.

So far, so good. But we have to remember at this place that, especially in the context of Western theological history, grace is a deeply problematic concept, having suffered a long existence semi-reified as a kind of causal agency midway between God and the creature (I parody, but not much). Robert Jenson's point about the aftermath of Augustine's rendering as 'functionally indistinguishable' the three persons of the Trinity is here pertinent:

> With the specifically Christian understanding of the relation between God and the faithful thus blocked, Augustine was left with the standard position of Western culture-religion [significantly, the very religion whose breakdown provided Hegel with his crisis]: on the one hand there is God, conceived as a supernatural entity who acts causally on us; and on the other there are the results of that causality upon us. In the subsequent Latin tradition, God and the objects of God's causality are then both interpreted accordingly: they are 'substances,' fundamentally self-sustaining and self-contained entities, who 'act' over against each other, the result of which action is in us a *habitus*, an acquired disposition to behave and react in ways obedient to the will of God.[21]

Barth's great achievement is relentlessly to turn this semi-causal notion of grace into a characterisation of personal divine action. 'We are concerned with the living person of Jesus Christ. Strictly, it is not grace, but He Himself as its Bearer, Bringer and Revealer, who is the Victory, the light which is not overwhelmed by darkness ...'[22] Grace is the event of God's gracious action towards and in the human agent. But, and here Barth does not much distinguish, there is a distinction to be made between gracious action christologically construed – in the becoming immanent that is incarnation – and divine action

---

[21] Robert W. Jenson, 'The Holy Spirit', *Christian Dogmatics*, edited by C. E. Braaten and R. W. Jenson (Philadelphia: Fortress Press, 1984), vol. 2, p. 126.
[22] Barth, *Church Dogmatics* 4/3, p. 173.

conceived pneumatologically and therefore eschatologically and transcendentally. It is this distinction that Barth generally fails to articulate in his treatment of the humanity of Christ in the second part of volume 4.

There are three symptoms which are worth mentioning, the first two belonging together. First, Barth asserts the *non posse peccare*, that Jesus was not able to sin;[23] and, second, in one of his rare allusions to the relation of the Spirit to Jesus he speaks in terms that suggest more causal compulsion than liberating for action. In one revealing statement he speaks of 'the Spirit who controls (*regieriende*) this man'.[24] A number of observations are here in order before we come to the third symptom. First, Barth does not fail to produce the necessary criticism of the Lutheran doctrine of the *communicatio idiomatum*, arguing that it is abstract, ignores the actual gospel history and compromises both the humanity and the deity of the Saviour.[25] He is right. If the divine being, action and consciousness so pervade the human being of the Saviour, the resources for characterising his action as free human action are suppressed. But might not the same or similar be suspected of the Spirit who 'controls this man'? Second, Barth realises that the Reformed answer to the Lutheran monophysite tendency also fails. In the light of Jenson's criticism that Christendom's conception of grace displaced the personal action of God the Spirit, it is worth quoting what Barth says:

> It was fatal that in this respect the older Reformed dogmaticians ... adopted in principle the same approach as the Lutherans ... And in terminology they had suspicious affinities to later mediaeval scholasticism. Thus they spoke of a *gratia habitualis*, or many such, imparted to the human nature of Jesus Christ by infusion. Habitus comes from *habere*, and therefore denotes possession. But grace is divine giving and human receiving.[26]

[23] Barth, *Church Dogmatics* 4/2, pp. 92–3.
[24] Barth, *Church Dogmatics* 4/2, p. 347, *Kirchliche Dogmatik* 4/2 (TV Zürich, 1978), p. 388. The word is, to be sure, quoted out of context ('*der diesen Menschen regierende, von ihm ausgehende, ihn bezugende* ...') Yet is not the use of such a word perhaps indicative of a weakness of pneumatology?
[25] Barth, *Church Dogmatics* 4/2, pp. 75–80.
[26] Barth, *Church Dogmatics* 4/2, pp. 89f.

This brings us to the third symptom of a failure of pneumatology, which is that the features of Jesus' ministry which really interest Barth are the ways in which Jesus' actions are godlike. 'The royal man of the New Testament tradition is created "after God" (κατα θεον). This means that as a man he exists analogously to the mode of existence of God' (p. 166). Speaking of the New Testament witness to the one who 'was and is the royal man Jesus of Nazareth' (p. 249), he summarises it under three heads.

> In the first part we considered ... its [the existence of the man Jesus as the Gospels saw it] sovereignty as an epiphany of the Lord ... In the second part we noted the correspondence and parallelism of his existence with that of God as the Gospels see and represent it ... Then in the third and most detailed part we understood his life-act as the self-representation of the new and redemptive actuality of the kingdom of God, His mighty activity in words and deed which in their common reach indicate and fulfil in ever-extending circles the irruption of this kingdom.[27]

Most of what Barth says in his treatment of the royal humanity of the Son of God is unexceptionable. It is what he does not say that causes the problems. He is not so interested in the way in which they are paradigmatically human, and, indeed, one has to search hard for any real interest in Jesus' action as free human action. In order to see what more is required, we shall begin by looking back on the two traditions of scholastic theology and appropriate from them the language of *habitus* or, perhaps better, disposition. Human beings do develop dispositions to act in one way or another. They take shape as what we call virtues and vices, another two concepts which are indispensable in their place. But there's the rub, to quote one of the most famous discussions of moral action ever written. We recall that systematic theology is not so much a matter of the organising of doctrines into systems, as of weighting and balance in the ways doctrinal matters are placed into relation with one another. Our question here is: what might greater attention to

---

[27] Barth, *Church Dogmatics* 4/2, pp. 248–9; one is inclined to suspect something of a *theologia gloriae* here.

the third person of the Trinity, more weight given to his action, enable us to say about the divine–human relation and in particular the forms of human action that eventuate from it?

The Holy Spirit is the agent of otherness and particularity, the one who realises the relation to one another of Father and Son in their very otherness. The Spirit is the Spirit of otherness in being the agent of the Son's movement out of the life of the Trinity to become the mediator of the Father's creating and redeeming action towards and in the world. The Spirit is the mediator of particularity in being the one who forms a body for the Son – *this* Jewish child of *this* Jewish mother – comes upon him in baptism, drives him into the wilderness to be tempted and there supports him so that he may become the particular Israelite that he was called to be and become. The Spirit is the one by whom the Father enables him to speak the truth, heal the sick and endure Gethsemane. It is not until his death that the Spirit is withdrawn, only to raise him from the dead and set him at the Father's right hand to be, until the end of time – but not of the kingdom – the mediator of the Father's rule and conquest of death. In sum, the Spirit is the mediator of the Son's relation to the Father in both time and eternity.

But he is also the one whose specific work in relation to the ascended Lord is to call into relation to God the Father through him a community to be his body in the world. That action takes a number of forms, the first and constitutive of which is election: the calling of particular persons into a form of relation-in-otherness that is known as κοινωνια, communion. Is it too much to speculate that the Spirit's primary redemptive work is in creating around the incarnate and ascended Son of God forms of being in relation – forms of communion – which, by realising the will of the creator for them, image in time the relation in love of the Father, Son and Spirit? Communion is accordingly a way of being human in relation to God – a relation constituted by God – which is at the same time in analogy or correspondence with God. For Hegel, to be sure, the Spirit's freedom enables the overcoming of otherness; for Christian theology, it consists in its realisation. The Spirit does not abrogate but realises particularity, in relation to others, but particularity none the less. And there is a contrast with Barth, too: redeemed human relations, that is to say, are not simply the forms of being which are analogous to the Son's relation to the Father, but are those that consist in being conformed to the human way of being of the Son, the second Adam, by the communion-creating action of the Spirit. Our theology of mediation and formation will follow from this: that a Christian ethic must first be conceived as those forms of right action which are enabled to take place by the Spirit as a function of the renewed relation to God taking shape in the community of worship and belief that is the body of Christ.

It is here that we come to the eschatological dimensions of ethics. If it is the Spirit's particular work to enable anticipations of that perfection promised for the end – anticipations of the heavenly communion – then among his works will be the constitution of right human actions. As we have seen, right human action arises from a redemptive relation to the creator, the God and Father of our Lord Jesus Christ. The Holy Spirit is, almost by definition, we might say, the one who enables this right relation to be realised. And here we take up Hegel's point. Freedom is the gift of the Spirit to the individual – I would prefer to say to the particular human person – but only in relation to other human agents. We are beings who by our actions either enable other human beings and the world to become that which they are created to be – in our context, to perform right actions – or fail so to enable them.[28]

Being formed Christianly is being conformed *to* Christ, *in* Christ in order that the former type of actions begin to displace the latter. Being in communion, we might say, is a *habitus* that has to be learned: there is, to allude to another Kierkegaard title, a *Training into Christianity*, and because all Christian action can only be more or less adequate anticipation of the end, it is never, short of that end, complete. The vertical relation is indeed the prior and determinative; but it is not realised apart

---

[28] Notice that there is already in this trinitarian analogy an implicit theology of the mission of the Church beyond itself. It has sometimes worried commentators that the ethical teaching of the Fourth Gospel appears to be interested almost entirely in inner-churchly relationships, in apparent neglect of the implications of John 1.14. But that is to miss the point. John is interested in the formation of Christians in the community because only through that does the effect of the stone tossed into the pool spread outward to the edges. See again Francis Watson, 'Trinity and Community: a Reading of John 17', *International Journal of Systemic Theology* 1 (1999), 167–83, p. 181.

from the horizontal. In place of the problematic concepts of uncreated and created grace, we therefore have a concept of the gracious action of God the Father by his Spirit in Christ and *consequently* in the communion of the body of Christ.[29] This does not, of course, exclude the action of the Spirit *extra muros ecclesiae*, but that is a question that is not at issue here. What is at issue is the meaning of divine grace, or, better, gracious divine action enabling, through Christ, particular human actions to be truly and freely human for the sake of the salvation of the world.

IV   *Conclusion*

A conclusion begins with two remarks. First, we have come a long way from Origen's view of theology as a tightly ordered doctrinal system. Much more strongly in focus is the notion of theology as seeking to make intelligible the *space* that God creates for human agents to realise authentically human forms of action. Second, in a conference dedicated to the theological relevance of Kierkegaard, more has been quarried from Hegel and Barth than from him. In terms of citations that is indeed the case. Yet he is the essential inspiration for a move from a scholastic to a more open conception of dogmatics. Important as is the rule of faith as a basis for theology, even more is it necessary to remember that it is a rule of *faith*; the articulation of a human response to divine action in Christ and the Spirit. Through the redeeming and enabling action of the two hands of God we reach a more open conception of dogmatics, but one that is also firmly structured by trinitarian considerations rather than by the drive to system which marks Hegel so indelibly, and is not always absent from Barth's more essentially Kierkegaardian orientation. So, let the Kierkegaard of *Fear and Trembling* have the last word in what he says about the Christian *habitus*: 'to change the leap of life into walking, absolutely to express the sublime in the pedestrian – only that knight [the knight of faith] can do it, and this is the one and only marvel.'[30]

---

[29] See, further, chapter 10 below.
[30] Kierkegaard, *Fear and Trembling*, p. 41.

CHAPTER 5

HOLINESS, DIFFERENCE AND THE ORDER OF CREATION

I *Continuity and holiness*

It is not much of an exaggeration to say that Karl Barth's dismissal of Rudolf Otto's concept of God's holiness amounts rather to saying that holiness is not a shudder down the spine.[1] Barth was right for a reason made clear by the book of Leviticus. In commanding Israel to be holy as God is holy, the book manifestly did not expect the analogous condition to consist in the *mysterium tremendum et fascinans*. In what then does the analogy consist? It is often suggested that holiness is to do with otherness, difference, that fashionable modern, or should I say postmodern, concept. '"Holy" describes the character of God ... *who is unapproachable because of his complete "otherness" and perfection when compared with all created things.*'[2] Yet a mark of the way in which the discussion of the nature of God has been dominated by philosophical treatments of the divine attributes is that a recent work on the topic makes only one reference to holiness, with a quotation from Norman Snaith to the effect that God is separate and distinct because he is God: separated

---

[1] Karl Barth, *Church Dogmatics*, translation edited by G. W. Bromiley and T. F. Torrance (Edinburgh: T. & T. Clark, 1957–1975), 1/1, p. 135, cf. 2/1, p. 360: 'The holy God of Scripture is certainly not "the holy" of R. Otto, that numinous element which, in its aspect as *tremendum*, is in itself and as such the divine. But the holy God of Scripture is the Holy One of Israel.' There is, to be sure, that side of it, as Isaiah 6 indicates. Leviticus 9.24, sometimes cited in this connection, is less Otto-esque: the people did prostrate themselves before God's glory, but only after 'shouting for joy'.

[2] Walter Eichrodt, *Theology of the Old Testament*, vol. 1, translated by J. A. Baker (London: SCM Press, 1961), p. 273. Italics in original.

to not *from.*[3] God is different, other as the creator is than the creature, and in that sense not to be compared at all. And yet that difference is to be mirrored, echoed, reflected, however we put it, in Israel's being among the nations.[4]

That, however, is only a beginning. In what does that difference consist? If the detailed regulations in Leviticus are taken out of context, some modes of behaviour are commanded which seem to us rather odd, if not worse, perhaps especially in a world marked by feminism. Let us, however, concentrate on the general question raised by this. Why, for example, do we no longer worry about wearing clothes made out of two different fabrics, while the New Testament and many believers continue to uphold its rejection of homosexual practices? The matter can also be illustrated by the matter of clean and unclean meat. Whether Peter's vision recorded in Acts 10 is meant to imply the end of Levitical food regulations – for the beasts in the sheet are clearly symbolic of classes of human being rather than of interest for themselves – it certainly casts doubt on the kind of classification that Leviticus presupposes. Mark 7.19 undoubtedly does, as do other significant episodes recorded in the gospels.[5] Yet the distinction between clean and unclean animals clearly does refer to something of immense theological importance, as Mary Douglas was among the first to realise. We are here concerned with that which does, and does not, conform to the order of creation, that which has been established by God to be what it distinctively is.[6]

And that brings us to our first important dogmatic conclusion from Leviticus' categories. The book presents a fallen world, in the respect at least that some of the beasts fail

<hr>

[3] M. Sarot and G. van den Brink, eds., *Understanding the Attributes of God* (New York: Lang, 1999), citing Norman Snaith, *The Distinctive Ideas of the Old Testament* (London: Epworth, 1944), p. 30.

[4] Ironically, the effect of Israel's difference has been to induce horror in her persecutors, not to mention the immediate effect of Jesus on some of his hearers, as Mark in particular is clearly anxious to point out. So perhaps Otto was not so far off the mark, in a way he perhaps did not imagine.

[5] For example Jesus' response to the woman who touched the hem of his robe suggests that he was at least sitting light to purity rules, Matt. 9.20–22.

[6] Mary Douglas, *Purity and Danger. An analysis of the concepts of Pollution and Taboo* (London: Ark Books, 1974), p. 53.

to conform to that which things were, in their integrity, created to be. And so it is with the New Testament, although the focus of clean and unclean is different, as we shall see. The dogmatic problem here is that of continuity, and, of course, the sensitive matter of supersession. What are the proper continuities? Why do I eat pork, without qualm except when what appears to be the merely moral concern over the conditions in which animals are reared intrudes itself? In turn that raises another question. Is vegetarianism merely a moral reaction to modern exploitation of the beast, or are there deeper currents, involving what is recognisably a concern for the kind of cleansing that is intrinsically related to a theology of sacrifice, with *holiness?* To complicate matters yet further, we must remember that, at least on Milgrom's interpretation, the cultic dispensation in Leviticus is fundamentally moral in orientation. 'The purification offering taught the ecology of morality, that the sins of the individual adversely affect society even when committed inadvertently ... The ethical thrust of these two expiatory sacrifices can be shown to be evident in other respects as well.'[7] And if deeper questions than the merely moral – as if there were such – are at stake, should we not ask what is holiness, at least for the sake of delimiting the subject, the holiness expected of or attributed to Christians? So, we have our enquiry, and it concerns the related problems of continuity and holiness. We shall begin with the problem of continuity.

The Christian tradition realised from the outset that something was changed in its apprehension of the law after Jesus. He had himself recommended a new way of looking at it, to say the least, interpreting or reinterpreting it with an authority that might appear to negate the tradition. For example Mark 7.14ff. could be interpreted as an attack on Leviticus' purity codes. Yet theological formulations of the situation have often failed to treat with due seriousness the indispensable part of the Old Testament in shaping a Christian understanding of the law. The notion, dating from early Christian times, that Jesus formulated a new law is dangerously subject to a supersessionist reading, and certainly

---

[7] Jacob Milgrom, *Leviticus 1–16* (London: Doubleday, 1991), p. 51. Milgrom evinces also the book's concern for the poor, and that 'the blood prohibition is an index of P's concern for the welfare of humanity', p. 47.

has been, indicating a besetting weakness of the tradition ever since. We shall approach the question by an examination of Calvin's nuanced and yet, I think, flawed treatment of the Old Testament law, which for him, as for Jesus, was the law of God, 'by whose coming nothing is to be taken away from the observance of the law'.[8] This non-supersessionist conception is linked with Calvin's return to what was Irenaeus's view of the relation of the Testaments. Both theologians, the father and the Reformer, share the view that the difference is quantitative rather than qualitative. Alluding to Matthew 13.52 – 'here is one greater than the temple' – Irenaeus comments: 'But *greater* and *less* are not applied to those things which have nothing in common between themselves, and are of an opposite nature, and mutually repugnant; but are used in the case of those of the same substance, and which possess properties in common, but merely differ in number and size ...'[9] Calvin is similar: 'The covenant made with all the patriarchs is so much like ours in substance and reality that the two are actually one and the same. Yet they differ in the mode of dispensation.'[10] One marked feature of Francis Watson's recent contributions to hermeneutics has been his sustained attack on the Marcionism which has marked much modern biblical interpretation. I hope that this chapter may serve to illuminate one aspect of this important question.[11]

II   *Calvin's continuity*

Consistent with his view of the single covenant, Calvin has a strongly positive view of Old Testament law, his exposition of the Decalogue being one of the most creative, as well as one of the longest, chapters of the *Institutes*.[12] It is in the chapter

---

[8] John Calvin, *Institutes of the Christian Religion*, edited by J. T. McNeill, translated and indexed by F. L. Battles, Library of Christian Classics, vols. 20 and 21 (Philadelphia: Westminster Press, 1960), II. vii. 14.

[9] 'Such as', he adds, 'water from water, and light from light, and grace from grace.' Irenaeus, *Against the Heresies*, 4. 9. 2.

[10] Calvin, *Institutes* II. x. 2.

[11] Francis Watson, *Text and Truth. Redefining Biblical Theology* (Edinburgh: T. & T. Clark, 1997).

[12] Calvin, *Institutes*, II. viii. Hereafter, references to the *Institutes* will appear in parentheses in the main text.

previous to that that he sets out his understanding of the relation between the two legal dispensations. His orientation means that Calvin is strong on continuity, particularly in the famous treatment of the third use of the law, the law as a guide for the Christian life. Here he conceives the law in terms of promise, and this is because he has a broad view of what is meant by law: 'I understand by the word "law" not only the Ten Commandments ... but the form of religion handed down by God through Moses' (II. vii. 1). Accordingly, Psalm 119 and the like, 'do not contradict Paul's statements' – which serve to make a different point – 'but proclaims the great usefulness of the law: the Lord instructs by their reading of it those whom he inwardly instils with a willingness to obey' (vii. 12). There is to be no rash rejection of Moses who, 'has admirably taught that the law ... ought among the saints to have a better and more excellent use', for: 'the law points out the goal toward which throughout life we are to strive' (vii. 13). Calvin similarly affirms, on the basis of Matt. 5.17–18 that: 'through Christ, the teaching of the law remains inviolable ...' (vii. 14). Even when he comes to the traditional and I believe essentially problematic assertion of the abolition of the 'ceremonies' he is more nuanced than a first reading might suggest. To be sure, he says that 'the holy patriarchs ... only glimpsed from afar and in shadowy outline what we see today in full daylight' (vii. 16). Yet: 'The ceremonies ... have been abrogated not in effect, but only in use. Christ by his coming has terminated them, but has not deprived them of anything of their sanctity ...' (vii. 16).

Calvin approaches the question of discontinuity through a discussion of the abolition of the 'written bond' of Colossians 2.14, attacking those who say that it is concerned with the mitigating of the severity of the moral law. It must rather refer to the ceremonies, which he takes to refer to 'ritual cleansings and sacrifices', for the author speaks of them as 'a wall that divides the Jews from the Gentiles', and he cites Augustine for the view that in the Jewish ceremonies there was confession of sins rather than atonement for them. But even that, he believes, is too superficial unless it is qualified, and Augustine also supplies him with the key to the discontinuity: it is not to be found in any of the outward characteristics of the dispensation, but 'the thing itself cries out that we should consider it as something more inward' (vii. 17).

In summary the following points need to be noted. First, as that chapter indicates, Calvin has, consonant, as is often pointed out, with his early training, a positive view both of law in general and of that contained in the Old Testament in particular. Second, he attempts to draw from Scripture as a whole his view of those items of Old Testament law which have in some way been superseded.[13] Prominent among his authorities here are the speech of Stephen and the Letter to the Hebrews – whose affinities he has noticed well in advance of modern scholarship – and, significantly, the prophets' denunciation of sacrifice. Third, in apparent agreement with 2 Corinthians, he contrasts the spiritual nature of the New Testament dispensation with something whose character is not quite clear. Again, there is ambiguity. His use of Hebrews is, consonant with one recurring strain of his theology, rather Platonising. Yet it also enables him to affirm the value of the apparently most superseded items of the Pentateuch, suggesting, for example, that there is something spiritual underlying the detailed instructions on the making of the tabernacle, without which Israel would have been 'just like the Gentiles are in their trifles'. It is in his appeal to inwardness which we met above that we find the heart of the problem, because it suggests a move away from a quantitative to a qualitative view of discontinuity: 'Yet that very type shows that God did not command sacrifices in order to busy his worshippers with earthly exercises. Rather, he did so that he might lift their minds higher' (vii. 1). 'Earthly exercises'? – such as, we might say if we wish to be carping, eating bread and drinking wine? Here his companion in arms, Irenaeus, was different.

Much, if not all, hangs on the meaning of that term so important to Calvin, 'spiritual', reflecting as it does his Augustinian inheritance. What is meant by that ambiguous, nay multivalent term? What is spiritual for a gnostic or an exponent of the so-called creation spirituality – if they can be distinguished – is not necessarily the same as that which is spiritual for the writer of Ezekiel 37, with his material and political

---

[13] This is not supersessionism in the strict sense because it is not Israel with whom we are concerned so much as one aspect of the Old Testament dispensation.

message. The ambiguity appears in Calvin because sometimes he contrasts spirit with letter, as sometimes does Paul, but sometimes, apparently, with matter, for instance in the statement we have met about 'earthly exercises'. Yet the sentences preceding that observation, falling somewhat short of Calvin's customary clarity, suggest that even here he is impatient with anyone who will disparage the old dispensation. They are worth hearing:

> Therefore, with good reason, both in Stephen's speech and in The Letter to the Hebrews very careful consideration is given to that passage where God orders Moses to make everything pertaining to the Tabernacle in accordance with the pattern shown to him on the mountain. For if something spiritual had not been set forth to which they were to direct their course, the Jews would have frittered away their effort in these matters, just as the Gentiles did in their trifles. Irreligious men ... cannot bear to hear about such complicated rites without aversion ... [Because] they do not pay attention to the purpose of the law; if the forms of the law be separated from its end, one must condemn it as vanity. (vii. 1)

The eschatological note that so marks Paul, and probably Hebrews, is there but muted, because, as so often in Calvin, there is a Platonic undertow which tends to a contrast between the spiritual and the material rather at the expense of a contrast of anticipation and fulfilment.

III   *Criteria of holiness*

In order to approach the eschatological dimension which Calvin has underplayed and which is one of the keys to this matter, we must take a diversion through the question of the order of creation – if, indeed diversion it is. The reason is this. Holiness is, as we have seen, a concept related to the crucial biblical distinction between the creator and the creation. The concerns of Leviticus are precisely that, for its provisions uniformly concern Israel's habitation of the creation as that involves sexual relations, bodily fluids, the fabric of clothing and the possession and cultivation of the land alike – all matters which, for all our differences from that era, are also at the heart of our moral and cosmic ecology. But order is a multivalent concept, and so much care is needed. As was mentioned earlier, it is one of the keys to difficult passages in Leviticus. Certain creatures may not be eaten because in some ways their form appears to be contrary to that of the 'natural' order of things. There has been a process of improper exchange, perhaps related to an interchange of attributes belonging to different spheres, such as the land and the water. (The concept of exchange will be important in the following discussion.) However, to use a concept like 'order of creation', with its overtones of a timeless cosmos – 'laws which never shall be broken …' – is not without problems. Let us approach it by means of its apparent correlative, disorder.

The distinction between clean and unclean beasts – and, more strongly, the distinction between forms of human action that are clean and unclean, holy and unholy – imply a disorder which has supervened upon creation's wholesome order. The sacrificial system must surely be understood at least in part as the divine dispensation for dealing with certain forms of disorder, human and cosmic alike, but, as Milgrom has argued, chiefly, if not solely, human. The priestly theology, he contends, represents an attack on a pagan cosmology in the interests of ethics centring both order and disorder on God's relation with his human creation. We are, therefore, even here dealing with a self-conscious distinction between various forms of order, what Milgrom characterises as the pagan, with its demonising of nature, and the biblical which is in that respect more anthropocentric. Pollution is the product of human sin, nothing else.

With the demise of the demons, only one creature remains with 'demonic' power – the human being. . . .

The Priestly theologians make use of the same imagery, except that the demons are replaced by humans. Humans can drive God out of the sanctuary by polluting it with their moral and ritual sins. . . .

This thoroughgoing evisceration of the demonic also transformed the concept of impurity. In Israel, impurity was harmless. . . .[14]

[14] Milgrom, *Leviticus*, p. 43.

Despite certain differences, minimized by this commentator, between priest and prophet in their specific diagnoses of the malady,[15] what is not in dispute is that malady there was and is. In one of his diagnoses, Paul, basing his analysis in a reference to the disrupted order of creation – 'they worshipped the creature instead of the creator' – observes the symptoms of the malady to take the form of, once again, exchange involving the distortion of the good order of the creation. There is a veritable litany of exchange: they 'exchanged the glory of the immortal God for images . . .'; 'they exchanged the truth of God for a lie . . .'; 'their women exchanged natural relations for unnatural ones.' (See also Ps. 106.20, Jer. 2.11, Hos. 4.7, the first two, and probably all of them, centring the sin on idolatry.) While we are often reminded that a word used in different contexts cannot be assumed to imply the same meaning, it is surely the case that the repeated ηλλαξαν, albeit with the added μετ- in the latter two instances, is deliberate. We all know, of course, that μεταλασσω becomes καταλλασσω in the outcome of that to which Paul is speaking, but that we shall leave on one side for now. For we have a problem, and we shall approach it by way of the law.[16]

One of the ways in which the disorder of the creation is addressed in the epistles, and, indeed, in aspects of Jesus' teaching recorded in the gospels, is by the reassertion and in some cases intensification of the original law: 'but I say to you'. The relation between old and new dispensations, however, is perhaps best examined through two focuses. The first is Acts 15, once widely represented as a compromise between a supposed Gentile freedom from the law and Jewish insistence on its retention. As Richard Bauckham and others have argued, however, it is almost certainly not that, but a decision firmly rooted in the tradition. The argument of James the brother of Jesus 'means that the Torah itself requires Gentile members of the eschatological people of God to keep these, but only

---

[15] Milgrom, *Leviticus*, pp. 482–5.

[16] Does Peter's vision, although not directly about that, implicitly affirm that this particular understanding of the creation is superseded; and that exchange now has to involve something more radical than the blood of bulls and goats?

these, four commandments ...'[17] We are here referred to Leviticus, for, as Bauckham comments, it is widely recognised that the terms of the decree are based on Leviticus 18–19, in part as that reappears in various prophetic writings. Add to this the fact that this particular decision is related to the theology of the presence of God in the temple, and it is possible to see why it took the form it did, based as it was on a widely practised exegetical method, linking the laws with the prophecies of Gentiles joining the eschatological people of God.[18]

The real presence – to use the terminology of Steiner's Maurice Lectures[19] – of Leviticus in New Testament moral teaching is equally prominent in 1 Corinthians, an echo of Leviticus 18.8 appearing in 1 Corinthians 5.1, at the very beginning of an extended treatment of behaviour appropriate for members of the young Christian community. The following chapter contains a passage which is widely held to represent in some respect a republication of the Decalogue, and we shall look at its context with eyes given by Milgrom's *Leviticus*. The context of our particular chapter is the appeal by church members to pagan law courts in the settlement of disputes internal to the Church. By so taking recourse, the members of the Church are leaving the sphere of the holy and risking themselves under the authority of the principalities and powers, which have been defeated by Christ but continue to exercise the remnants of their power. That is to say, they are returning themselves to the sphere of the demonic from which they have been rescued. This represents an interesting inversion of Leviticus' demythologising of the demonic: like the pagan gods of 1 Cor. 8, the demonic realm may not *be real*, but that does not prevent it from, like the spirits of the Greek

---

[17] Richard Bauckham, 'James and the Jerusalem Church', Richard Bauckham, ed., *The Book of Acts in its Palestinian Setting* (Carlisle: Paternoster and Grand Rapids: Eerdmans, 1995), p. 452. It is the Noahide laws which are here the main obligation of Gentile converts: prohibited are idolatry, blasphemy, theft, sexual immorality, eating flesh or blood from a living animal.

[18] Bauckham, 'James and the Jerusalem Church', p. 460.

[19] George Steiner, *Real Presences. Is There Anything in What We Say?* (London: Faber & Faber, 1989).

underworld, being given a kind of existence by having its veins filled with blood.

This consideration leads Paul first into a general assertion that the wicked will put themselves outside the Kingdom of God, which is the place where runs the writ of the somewhat expanded summary of the Decalogue: 'no fornicator or idolater, no adulterer or sexual pervert, no thief, extortioner, drunkard, slanderer or swindler will possess the kingdom of God.' I know that the translation of the various terms for sexual sins is disputed,[20] but that is not to the point here, which is that just as for Leviticus the Torah delimits a sphere within which Israel exercises her calling to be holy as God is holy, so it is for this community. In Paul's remarks on sexual ethics which follow there are other parallels with Leviticus. Let us use Milgrom again to set the scene. Asking about the limited range of bodily secretions regarded by Leviticus as impure – for example 'mucus, perspiration, and, above all urine and feces' are not regarded as impure – he seeks an answer to the question of criteria through a broader enquiry about the phenomena that are regarded as sources of impurity, 'corpse/carcass, scale disease and genital discharges'. According to him 'there is a common denominator to the three above-mentioned sources of impurity – death ... The wasting of the body, the common characteristic of the highly visible, biblically impure scale disease, symbolizes the death process as much as the loss of vaginal blood and semen.'[21] What makes for life and what for death? That is surely the central criterion of ethical continuity between the Testaments – if, without further specification, unhelpfully vague.

Paul's equivalent in this context is this: theologically, there is a close connection between Jesus' resurrection, the believer's and the seriousness of what Christians do in and with their bodies. 'God not only raised our Lord from the dead; he will also raise us by his power. Do you not know that your bodies are limbs and organs of Christ ...'? It would be surprising if there is not in Paul's mind Jesus' reaffirmation of the teaching about

[20] Compare the more neutral REB rendering – influenced as it seems to be by a concern to distance the text from modern conceptions – with the NIV's 'nor male prostitutes nor homosexual offenders'.

[21] Milgrom, *Leviticus*, p. 46.

becoming 'one flesh' in sexual relations, and there is indeed
direct reference to Genesis 2.24. There is no trace of the
modern gnostic belief that we are genderless monads
imprisoned in a body which we may or may not acknowledge,
that we 'choose' our sexuality. Gilbert Meilaender puts it well:

> The body is the place of our personal presence. And moral
> significance must therefore be found not only in the spirit
> that characterises our relationships with others, not only in
> mutuality and communion, but also in the bodily relation-
> ship itself. To suppose that mutual love is all that is needed
> to make a relationship right is to ignore the moral signifi-
> cance of the body. It is, in fact, a kind of dualism that
> separates our true self from the body. If we want to know how
> rightly to use the body, therefore, if we want to distinguish
> between fulfilling and corrupting sexual relationships, we
> cannot talk only of love, consent, and mutuality.[22]

Paul seems to be reflecting the view of Scripture generally that
there is a respect in which we *are* our bodies, as male and
female, so that the purity teaching is not denied but fiercely
concentrated on the use of the body for the end for which it was
created.

> Human sexual desire ranges across a continuum, and the
> moral question is not why our desires draw us in one
> direction or another, but what behavior is right or wrong.
> The diversity of sexual desire in our world is, it turns out, very
> like the world Paul knew, with a kaleidoscopic variety of
> sexual desires and behaviors.[23]

To put it otherwise: among the fruits of redemption is the
proper relational use of the body. In reply to claims for
freedom from the law, Paul makes the point that the Christian
must not be mastered by anything, whether food or sex. The
reason is that 'the body is for the Lord and the Lord for
the body' (1 Cor. 6.13). The latter is particularly important,
for the resurrection of Jesus is the guarantee of the resurrection

---

[22] Gilbert Meilaender, 'The First of Institutions', *Pro Ecclesia* 6 (1997),
444–55, p. 446.
[23] Meilaender, 'The First of Institutions', p. 453.

of Paul's readers, and therefore of the body's importance. Moreover, the resurrection makes us 'members of Christ himself'. And there is no christology without pneumatology: 'your body is a temple of the Holy Spirit.' And the appeal to redemption returns at the end of the chapter: 'you were bought at a price. Therefore honour God with your body.'

It is at this place that we find the holiness teaching of the epistle. Paul expects his readers to be different, not to conform themselves to the ways of the pagan world, and what we discover is a further reinforcement of what Milgrom found in Leviticus' ethical construction of holiness and possibly also a development of the kind of considerations which drove the decision of Acts 15. Thus do we appear to have achieved the ultimate banality: holiness consists in conformity to the law. If I attempt to identify the uneasiness which the ethics of John Howard Yoder sometimes generates, it is to be found here, though banality would be the last accusation to level at such an influential thinker.[24] Yet the question insistently raises its head: Is this where our revision of Calvin leads – into Anabaptism? Let us look a little more deeply at what is happening in this chapter of 1 Corinthians.

According to the supporting theology, holiness is not first of all something to do, but a gift. Numerous New Testament epistles are addressed to οι αγιοι, and it is not a moralistic address. This chapter also makes clear that not ethics but their new basis is the case. 'You were like that', he tells his readers, but are no more: 'you were washed, you were sanctified, you were justified.' There is a clear parallel here to the argument of Romans 6, that because Christians are united with Christ, they should offer themselves to God, 'as those who have been brought from death to life' (1 Cor. 6.13). We are in the realm not merely of ethics, but of sacrifice and purity. Gordon Fee's argument that the reference to washing contains no more than an indirect allusion to baptism may well be right. Transformation through Christ and the Spirit – anticipation of

---

[24] I am not convinced that for all its orientation to worship, John Howard Yoder, *Body Politics. Five Practices of the Christian Community before the Watching World* (Nashville, Tennessee: Discipleship Resources, 1997) finally avoids the kind of moralism that directs the attention more to the community's practices than to its orientation to God in Jesus.

the eschatological transformation (1 Cor. 15.51: αλλαγησομεθα
– from μετα- to κατα- to αλλασσω) through the exchange
realised in the atonement – is surely what is in view, and Fee
comments that once again, as so often in this letter, Paul is
urging the Corinthians to become what they are.[25] Here we
come across the heart of the process of exchange which
reverses that of the improper exchange which brings about
disorder by subverting God's purposes for his creation. Calvin
hits the nail on the head in his exposition of this passage, again
implicitly recognising echoes of the conceptuality of Leviticus:

> Paul uses three expressions to convey the one idea ... His
> point is that once they have been justified they must not
> bring themselves into a new state of guilt; having been
> sanctified they must not make themselves unclean again;
> having been washed, they must not sully themselves with
> fresh filth ... [I]n this passage, the apostle's only purpose was
> to express himself in more than one way in magnifying the
> grace of God, which has delivered us from bondage to sin, so
> that we may learn from this how much we ought to shrink
> from everything that stirs up the anger and vengeance of God
> against us.[26]

While we may wish to take issue with the way the final phrase is
expressed, we surely may not deny the general point, which
is that, for Paul, although it is indeed the case that holiness is
the Christian calling, that is the fruit of a prior being made
holy, or reconciliation. That the ethical teaching of this epistle
cannot in any case be separated from the life of the community
of worship is manifest from the interrelation of sacrament and
morality in chapter 11. I will return briefly to this point below.

IV   *Eschatological concentration*

If anything is clear it is that disorder cannot be removed simply
by reasserting an ancient order; by being, in political terms,

[25] Gordon D. Fee, *The First Epistle to the Corinthians* (Grand Rapids: Eerdmans, 1987), p. 247.
[26] John Calvin, *The First Epistle of Paul the Apostle to the Corinthians*, edited by D. W. Torrance and T. F. Torrance (Grand Rapids: Eerdmans, 1960), pp. 126–7.

reactionary. The lurking danger, represented by Calvin's ambiguity about the meaning of 'spiritual', is always of a contrast between the material and the spiritual, symbolised as it is in the concept of the ceremonial law. Lost is the eschatological orientation whose reintroduction makes a number of moves possible. In the first place, it enables a discussion of those things which are superseded by Christ without thereby falling into supersessionism. In the second place, and more important for our purposes, it enables a more satisfactory discussion of the continuity and discontinuity between Old Testament and New Testament law. We cannot evade either the fact that something is new, something is superseded and that, in some respect difficult to define, gospel is prior to law. The point is this: if we identify, as Calvin sometimes seems to do, the spiritual with the inward and non-material, we obtain too easy a solution of the problem of discontinuity. The prophets' and even the Epistle to the Hebrews' attitude to the cult becomes the occasion for a moralising or spiritualising which severs the lifeline, the continuity between the Testaments so well expressed by Calvin most of the time. In other words we need a third programmatic conception to supplement and relate the two we have used so far, of the order and disorder of creation. That, I want to suggest, is concentration. The relation between old and new law is not supersession, not spiritual against material, but enrichment and concentration of the orientation to God-given life that is there from the beginning. The life and death which bulked so large in the priestly writings are now concentrated on cross and resurrection of Jesus: put to death for our sins, raised for our justification. We have seen how important for the concept of disorder, of fall, is the notion of a false exchange. Disorder can be removed not by repristination but by an exchange of the old for the new.

We come, then, to καταλλασσω which displaces the μεταλλασσω which has been the source of unholiness, the disruption of the right relation between holy creator and that which is to be holy as he is holy. Whether or not he uses the same terminology as Paul, this is the theme of the author to the Hebrews, where there is an extended treatment of reconciliation as concentration: the concentration of the relation between God and the world in the person and work of Jesus, whose 'blessed exchange' is, according to the Letter to Diognetus, similarly concentrated. 'O sweetest exchange ... The sinfulness of many is hidden in the righteous one, while the righteousness of the One justifies the many that are sinners.'[27] Holiness is the fruit – first fruits! – of the crossing over of the Son of God into the realm of the profane, *meaning* the realm of those who lose the glory of God by worshipping the creature instead of the creator. If the presence of God was once in some way realised – concentrated – in tabernacle, temple, land, law and people, it is now concentrated in this one Jew, who becomes them all, and, in our context, specifically, becomes Torah that is to say, the mediator – as the ascended Lord – of the presence of God on earth. Undoubtedly the best elaboration of this is to be found in the Letter to the Hebrews, according to which the meaning and reality of the sacrificial – 'ceremonial' – system are concentrated in the one who was made perfect through what happened to him. '[W]hen this priest had offered for all time one sacrifice for sins, he sat down at the right hand of God.' The following verse returns us, significantly, to something remarkably like the eschatology of 1 Corinthians, linking ascension and eschatology in almost identical terms. 'Since that time he waits for his enemies to be made his footstool, because by one sacrifice he has made perfect for ever those who are being made holy'(Heb. 10.12–14).

In the latter phrase is to be found the eschatological dialectic which is the key to the meaning of the holiness of the creature in relation to that of God. 'He has made perfect those who are being made holy'; is this not exchangeable with: 'he has made holy those who are being made perfect?' Neither the present nor the perfect tense is separable from the other, nor from the fact that the last enemy to be overcome is death. We return to that which Leviticus and the New Testament have in common: a concern with life and death. For Paul the horror of recourse to pagan courts, of incest, of the continuing of social and economic divisions at the eschatological supper – in sum, of all behaviour whose persistence excludes its perpetrators from the

[27] 'The So-Called Letter to Diognetus', edited and translated by Eugene R. Fairweather, in Cyril C. Richardson, ed., *Early Christian Fathers*, Library of Christian Classics 1 (London: SCM Press, 1953), pp. 205–24, p. 221.

Kingdom (and compare Rev. 22.15) – derives from the fact that alike they make for death and not life, that they take those who have been made holy out of the realm, the sphere of influence, of the crucified and risen Jesus. It is eschatology that makes all the difference: the bearing not of the order of creation but of its promised redemption from vanity to the liberty of the children of God.

And here we come to the weakness of Calvin's account of the difference between old law and new. It is indeed a case of the priority of the 'spiritual'; but that does not mean the abolition of 'ceremonies' but their *concentration*: their focusing on highly physical things, like the relations of embodied men and women and the sharing of bread and wine. Leviticus knew that too. But christology must make all the difference, for this is an unusual priest, with unusual ways of concentrating the law and the prophets.

V   *Coda*

To be holy is to be different; for Israel from the peoples around, and for the New Testament people of God from the social order in which it is set. Here we can agree with Yoder, Hauerwas and company. Is that a form of the 'sectarianism', of which those theological moralists are so often accused? Perhaps it is if the decisive difference – the *qualitative* – difference is the ethical. But it cannot be. After all, the Gentiles sometimes do what the law commands rather more successfully than the elect children of the Kingdom. Eschatologically, perhaps the difference between the two overlapping and interacting worlds is but numerical like that between the dispensations of the one covenant.[28] That is, to be sure, a real difference: between those who are seeking by their patterns of life together to become what they are and those who are not. What, then, is the heart of the difference between Church and world? Surely it is in the ceremonies, those anticipations of the eschatological banquet which are the community's sacrifice of praise. When the

---

[28] Possibly all will be made holy in the end, as some interpretations of Romans 11 might encourage us to think.

orientation is to worship, the law falls into place as the action which flows from a reconciled relation to God in Christ made concrete – concentrated? – by the Spirit in word, baptism, and Lord's Supper.[29]

---

[29] It is surely worth noting that for Paul the 'logical' act of worship is the offering of the bodies of the faithful as a *living* sacrifice – not being 'conformed to the pattern of this world ...' (Rom. 12.1–2).

CHAPTER 6

THE CHURCH AS A SCHOOL OF VIRTUE?

Human Formation in Trinitarian Framework[1]

Contributing to the rediscovery of the centrality of the virtues for human being is one of the gifts of inestimable value that Stanley Hauerwas has given to the world. There is no escaping the concept of virtue, even though much modern moral philosophy and theology has sought to do so, with its individualistic idea of the person as naked, choosing will: the rootless I of existentialism and consumerism. Perhaps central amongst Hauerwas' contributions is to remind us that we are creatures who have our being in time, and that the temporal, or narrative, shape of our being is intrinsic. 'The virtues are timeful activities. This is not just because the virtues can only be developed through habitual formation, but because the virtues bind our past with our future by providing us with continuity of self.'[2] How are our selves formed in time? In this chapter, it will be contended that an ethic of virtue need not be incompatible with a doctrine of justification, as is sometimes suggested by both Hauerwas and others. Without wanting to deny that we need the virtues, I hope to place the notion in the context of a doctrine of God, giving it a broader basis than it sometimes has. Some of the questions I am following up have been suggested to me by Ellen Charry's recent book, and here I want to argue first, in agreement, for the necessity of a doctrine of the

---

[1] First delivered at a Theological Convocation at Bangor Seminary, Maine, in January 1999. This version was adapted as a contribution to a *Festschrift* for Stanley Hauerwas.

[2] Stanley Hauerwas, *Christian Existence Today* (Durham: NC: Labyrinth Press, 1988), p. 265.

101

immanent Trinity, and then enquire into the way in which such a doctrine might feed an understanding of what it is to be human.[3] The path there, however, is tortuous, somewhat as follows.

First will come an outline of a trinitarian doctrine of creation, which is needed for an understanding of the framework for being a human being in the wider created order. Then, second, there will follow an introduction to the notion of virtue, and particularly in relation to human sinfulness. What are we to make of virtue in a fallen world? Third, 'Remaking the human', will say something about salvation as the act of the triune God, and the way in which God's action in the economy is based in God's eternal triune being. Fourth, something will be said about the place of the Church in the formation of human virtues. In all the sections a double question will form a background accompaniment: what is the relation between being – what God and we are – and act? Do our acts flow from our being, as is the emphasis of an ethic of virtue, of training people to be certain kinds of people, so that certain kinds of acts follow from what they are? Or is the act more important, so that we form our persons from what we do? That is on the whole a more typical modern view, although it is, of course, a much more complicated matter than that makes it seem. The two are so interdependent that it scarcely seems possible to disentangle them, so that the main question for us is: how might the Church be conceived to play a part in shaping the being of people so that they are free to act in a way that makes for life rather than for death?

I *God, creation and eschatology*

On the relation of the economic and immanent Trinity, there is just a little to be said. Rather than presenting yet another discussion of what has come to be called Rahner's rule, I would here simply repeat the procedure of Karl Barth on the relations of the revealed and ontological Trinity: that one

---

[3] Ellen Charry, *By the Renewing of your Minds. The Pastoral Function of Christian Doctrine* (New York and Oxford: Oxford University Press, 1997).

cannot say of the eternal being of God more than is licensed by his revelation. It does not however follow that, as is sometimes concluded, God is only the economy. Barth's and, more ambiguously, Rahner's proposal is that while economy betokens being – what God does reveals who he is – being is by no means reduced to it. The point of affirming an immanent Trinity in *relative* distinction from the economic is to allow for personal space between God and the world. If God does not enable the world to be other because and in as much as he is other than it, the being of the world risks being simply swallowed up in that of God. At this place, the doctrine of the Trinity and the ontology of creation it involves perform a crucial and necessary function. By showing that it is one thing to be God, another to be the world, they enable both to be themselves, in right relation. That is a far more important rule than Rahner's because any breach risks binding the world so much into God's being that it loses its own distinctive reality.

Why? Only if God has freedom of action do we also. To be sure, there is freedom and freedom: freedom as the modern world tends to conceive it, as individual autonomy, an indelible character of the person, unaffected or relatively unaffected by relation to others; and a more relational and biblical conception. Here a number of questions jostle for attention, including one that would perhaps take us too far afield, that of the sense in which we would wish to say that God is free.[4] Our question is that of human formation, and in respect to freedom the question is: are we formed in freedom, or are we in some way automatically free? And if we have to be formed in freedom, does this involve that notion with which the modern world is most uncomfortable, that we have to receive our freedom from outside, from others?[5] Suppose that we examine the question with the help of the notion of autonomy. Autonomy appears to require that human beings are self-directed, in the strongest sense of being utterly responsible for the formation of our ethical principles and actions. What place here is there for *being formed*? Yet in assuming that that is what

---

[4] See Robert W. Jenson, 'An Ontology of Freedom in the *De Servo Arbitrio* of Luther', *Modern Theology* 10 (1994), 247–52, p. 250.
[5] This question is treated in detail in chapters 9 and 10 below.

autonomy involves, we are begging a question, that namely of what autonomy *means*. What is the law of our being? Indeed, what are we *ourselves*? Let me begin with the general question, already touched on, of the real and distinct existence of things in general before moving to people.

The key is to be found in that most disputed and often neglected of doctrines, that of the Holy Spirit. So dominated have we been with what can be called the religious functions of the Spirit – the early theologians, for example, often defended his divinity by appeal to little more than the fact that sanctification is a divine work – that we tend to forget that the Spirit is the lord and giver of life universally. Insofar as we can distribute forms of action among the persons of the Trinity, Basil of Caesarea should be our guide. While affirming that the Holy Spirit is 'inseparable and wholly incapable of being parted from the Father and the Son', he yet held that it is necessary to distinguish: 'the original cause of all things that are made, the Father; ... the creative cause, the Son; ... the perfecting cause, the Spirit.'[6] I would gloss: the Father originates; he creates through the Son; and he perfects through the Spirit. What we gain is the notion of the Spirit as the perfecting cause, something Calvin picked up, saying of the Spirit that: 'in transfusing into all things his energy, and breathing into them essence, life, and movement, he is indeed plainly divine.'[7] Now perfecting might involve a number of things; two in particular. First, Calvin's point stresses the nature of the creating act: God sees all that he has made, and it is very good (Gen. 1), because it is perfected by the Spirit. In that sense, it is through the Spirit's action that we discern the basis of the world's distinction from God, its being itself, the world. As the 'perfecting cause' the Holy Spirit, the Lord and Giver of Life, gives reality to *the world* by perfecting what the Father does through his Son: originating what is truly other. Yet, because it is through the Son, the one who was to become incarnate, that the world was originated, it is not what it is outside a continuing relation to God.

The notion of a continuing relation of the world to its creator

[6] Basil of Caesarea, *On the Holy Spirit*, XV. 36 and 38.
[7] John Calvin, *Institutes of the Christian Religion*, edited by J. T. McNeill, translated and indexed by F. L. Battles, Library of Christian Classics, vols. 20 and 21 (Philadelphia: Westminster Press, 1960), I. xiii. 14.

brings us to the second way in which the Spirit is perfecting cause. This is in the eschatological action according to which the creation is finally brought to its perfection, its completedness, in the fullness of time. A side-swipe at one of the exponents of 'economy alone' trinitarians, Catherine Mowry LaCugna, will indicate something of what I mean. In one crucial passage, the author speaks of an

> emanation and return ... [which] express ... the one ecstatic movement of God outward by which all things originate from God through Christ in the power of the Holy Spirit, and all things are brought into union with God and returned to God. There is neither an economic nor an immanent Trinity; there is only the *oikonomia* that is the concrete realization of the mystery of *theologia* in time, space, history and personality.[8]

The question raised here is so important that I must spell out its implications. An eschatology of this kind, with its suggestion of a symmetrical outflow and return of things from and back to God, risks suggesting the ultimate pointlessness of creation. Is the world made simply to return to the nothingness whence it came? That is certainly the suggestion of much eschatology since Origen, and of Western eschatology since Tertullian in particular.[9] Against this, a truly pneumatological eschatology will allow us to pay far more attention to the creation's interest for and in itself: to give more stress both to its particular reality as this universe, the one created by God *for a purpose*, and to the being of the particular things and persons of which it is constituted. To be sure, we are not yet here in the realm of freedom, but giving human freedom foundation in the fact that the Spirit confers otherness on things, the fact that things are created for an end which is something more than is given in the beginning. Creation through the Spirit is creation that has a *telos*. To use an analogy from the arts, a block of marble is in its own way perfect; but in the hands of a sculptor, it is also *perfectible*.

The topic of this chapter is the eschatological destiny –

---

[8] Catherine Mowry LaCugna, *God for Us. The Trinity and Christian Life* (New York, HarperCollins, 1991), p. 223.
[9] Tertullian, *Against Hermogenes*, 34.

perhaps better, destination – of one part of the created order, the personal. Are human beings made to go somewhere – and if so, how do we get there? More elegantly, do we have a destiny, and how is it to be realised? To pursue our enquiry, we need to look at the one (particular!) human person who is what he was created to be. What makes Jesus the particular person that he is? The answer is to be found in his relation to Israel and Israel's God realised through the Spirit. That is the point of the gospel stories of his birth: as the eternal Son of God he becomes the son of this particular mother by the Spirit's recreating act; as this particular Israelite he is driven by the Spirit into the wilderness to test his messianic calling against other possibilities, and, by virtue of his obedient choice empowered by that Spirit to tell the truth, drive out the demons and in general re-establish God's rule; and raised from the dead as the first born of many brothers and sisters who become the Church. Some words of that great theologian of the humanity of Christ, the author to the Hebrews, make the point: 'he learned obedience from what he suffered' (5.8), a reference surely not to the cross alone, but to his whole life as it so culminated. We might gloss: he learned obedience through what happened to him, through what he experienced, went through. It was thus that he was 'made perfect' – Mary's child perfected through life and death and resurrection – something we must surely construe by reference to the eschatological perfecting of the Holy Spirit. Despite the paucity of direct references to the Spirit's activity – because of the essential self-effacingness of the Spirit's action, his activity has often to be read between the lines of Scripture – this letter has sometimes been argued to originate as a pentecostal address. At a crucial stage there is explicit pneumatology, and it comes in connection with Jesus' perfecting: 'who through the eternal Spirit offered himself unblemished to God ...' (9.14). If it is indeed the case that the Father sends him, as is the overall message of the New Testament, it is equally the case that his painfully achieved sinlessness derives from the Holy Spirit's maintaining him in relation to his Father. The perfection of Jesus' life *as a whole* consists in its conforming, realised by his relation to the Father through the Spirit, to that which he was created to be, to his particular *telos*. What we make of that, however, is somewhat complicated, and requires a little more analysis of our terms.

II *Human virtue in a fallen world*

So far one concept in particular has been considered, that of perfection, and particularly the characteristic action of the Holy Spirit in realising it. We now approach a second: that of virtue. In relating virtue and perfection, I want to take a risky and speculative step, combining Aristotle with some hints from Karl Barth, who, it may be remembered, resisted talk of God's attributes, preferring rather to speak of his perfections.[10] Perfections are the ways God both is and acts, both in his triune eternity and in relation to the world. God's grace and mercy, justice and holiness are God in action, and so are, we might say, the divine virtues in the exercise of which God is himself and not another. It is almost as if Barth were speaking of God's perfections as his virtues according to Aristotle's definition of virtue as a *hexis proairetike* (a settled disposition in exercising choice?).[11] God's 'virtues' are God in the perfect coincidence of being and act. This, we might say, is God's *character*, the settled shape of what he is and does.

May such an Aristotelian notion be applied by analogy to the human sphere? Can we speak in all this of the formation of Jesus' 'character', of his exercising 'virtues'? Luke certainly thinks so, for according to him the young Jesus was subject to his parents and 'grew in wisdom and stature, and in favour with God and men' (Luke 2.52). He would certainly appear to exercise what we would call virtues, even if not always in Aristotelian form: courage, truthfulness and love, if not impassibility, were Jesus' settled disposition, as the narrative depicts them. We can then understand human virtues, and certainly Jesus' virtues, as human perfections. His life as a whole is offered to God perfect because his *hexis*, his settled disposition, is determined by his relation to God the Father through the perfecting Spirit. How easily can this pattern be applied to our situation?

Here we reach the first difficulty we must surmount if we are

[10] Karl Barth, *Church Dogmatics*, translation edited by G. W. Bromiley and T. F. Torrance (Edinburgh: T. & T. Clark, 1957–1975), 2/1, §29.

[11] Aristotle, *Ethics*, 1106b36. Indeed, *proairesis* might well be a way of characterising both election and providence according to Barth's scheme of things.

to root what we say in the life of the Church. Human virtues are habits of the heart, in the sense that they are dispositions rooted in the fundamental orientation of the human agent. In our liberal culture we tend to think of acts as the undetermined effects of individual acts of will, forgetting that there is no act of will which does not arise out of a history, including a history of habitual behaviour. Let me illustrate with an extreme but illuminating case. In the second decade of last century, Samuel Taylor Coleridge performed two acts whose meanings are inseparable. He professed orthodox trinitarian belief and made confession of his addiction to opium, a drug he had taken originally for medical reasons. His addiction – his enslaving *habit* – gave him insights into the universal human condition which represent a modern republication of Augustine's anti-Pelagian arguments:

> By the long Habit of the accursed poison my Volition (by which I mean the faculty *instrumental* to the Will, and by which alone the Will can realise itself – its Hand, Legs, & Feet, as it were) was completely deranged ... and became an independent faculty.[12]

The distinction between the will and acts of volition is important: between that which we would do, and that which, as Coleridge shows, we actually do in acts of volition. Our will and our acts of willing have to be distinguished, because to be fallen is to act in a way that one essentially – that is to say, eschatologically – is not. 'For I have the desire to do what is good, but I cannot carry it out. For what I do is not the good I want to do; no, the evil I do not want to do – this I keep on doing' (Rom. 7.18b–19). What we call acts of will take shape in the heart, the settled disposition of the personal agent. Disable that, and the acts of volition become not only misdirected, as Coleridge realises in what is in effect a rehearsal of the argument of Romans 7, but actively work against the wishes of the heart.

---

[12] Cited by Richard Holmes from S. T. Coleridge, *Letters* III, pp. 489–90, in *Coleridge. Darker Reflections* (London: HarperCollins, 1998), pp. 356f. Coleridge continues: 'I used to think St James' Text, "He who offended in one point of the Law, offended in all", was very harsh; but my own sad experience has taught me its awful, dreadful Truth.' For a further use of this text, see below, chapter 9, pp. 164–5.

In sum: an ethic of virtue is good in that it makes possible a criticism of the anthropology of pure will that underlies so many modern characterisations of the person, and its accompanying view of acts as merely punctiliar, single acts without relation to past and present. Actions flow from and manifest being. But insofar as that being can be badly formed, and, indeed, according to the doctrine of sin, is badly formed, an ethic of virtue cannot be sufficient apart from a theology of redemption. Apart from redemption action does not correspond to eschatological destiny, but negates it. If, then, autonomy refers to the law of our being, that law must be understood eschatologically, with reference to what we are created to become, to the perfection to which we are called. This is an Irenaean theme: Adam and Eve's childlike nature implies a growth to maturity; but our fallenness, our turning backwards, requires the incarnation, death and resurrection of the eternal Son of God if a way forward is to be found. Does Stanley Hauerwas fail to emphasise satisfactorily this aspect of the matter, or is he in danger of an exemplarism of the cross, an implicit Pelagianism which lays upon human agents a burden too great for them to bear? I leave it as a question, and am, I think, not alone in doing so.

III *Remaking the human*

Ellen Charry has rightly criticised those who oppose the being and the act of God, advocating as they do 'a modern understanding of personhood that embraces growth and change and views personhood as constituted by action, not character'.[13] Of course it is a mistake to read into God's eternity categories taken from a temporal and fallen world. But a developmental view of created persons is inescapable. The three-personed God creates persons who are not eternal, but are made to have their being in time, as Stanley Hauerwas reminds us. They are finite and, as created, both mortal and directed to an end which exceeds their beginning, as the mature adult exceeds the child. 'Person' is an eschatological concept, so an eschatologically

---

[13] Charry, *Renewing*, p. 125.

oriented conception of the human involves training in virtue –
in human perfections.

Further, human characters need change because we are
fallen beings. This means that our character – our settled disposition – is such that our acts flow as much from vices as from
virtues, sometimes more. Character and act belong inseparably
together: the slavery at the heart of our being determines the
wrongness of our acts, and can be broken only by redemption.
The enemy is not action versus character, but the modern view
that life is constituted more by *decision* than through character;
or rather that our decisions come somehow out of the blue,
unrelated to the kind of people that we are. There Hauerwas is
absolutely right. To give centrality to decision is to make two
mistakes: it is to treat life as a series of points; and is to throw
too great a weight on a certain conception of human autonomy
at the expense of grace. In this respect, we cannot evade the
fact that apart from redemption, our virtues will be but shadows
of what they should be. That means, however, that we need not
accept a disjunction between a more Reformation-oriented
dialectic of *simul justus et peccator* and a more Methodist ethic of
virtue.[14] Renewal of character is based in God's reconciling act
in Christ, so that, as Calvin knew, we need to find room in our
theology for both sanctification and justification.[15]

That takes us back to the doctrine of the Trinity. To gain as
clear as possible a view of all the elements which must be held
in proper relative weight, we must retain in careful juxtapo-
sition the way we relate being and act in God and in human
agents. We have seen that, for Barth, God's perfections constitute the utter consistency of his being and act. We turn now
to the way in which God's act, rooted in his being, serves to
redirect human being to its proper end. Here Irenaeus, as
always in these matters, helps us, especially in one remarkable
chapter:

[God's] only-begotten Word, who is always present with the
human race, united to and mingled with His own creation,

---

[14] For a careful account of his position, see the new Introduction to Stanley
Hauerwas, *Character and the Christian Life* (Notre Dame: University of Notre
Dame Press, 1994, pp. xxixf.
[15] See chapter 7, below.

according to the Father's pleasure, and who became flesh, is Himself Jesus Christ our Lord, who did also suffer for us, and arose again on our behalf, and who will come again in the glory of His Father, to raise up all flesh. . . . There is therefore . . . one God the Father, and one Christ Jesus, who came by means of the whole dispensational [economic?] arrangements . . . and gathered together all things in Himself . . . [S]o that as in super-celestial, spiritual and invisible things, the Word of God is supreme, so also in things visible and corporeal He might possess supremacy, and, taking to Himself the pre-eminence, as well as constituting Himself Head of the Church, He might draw all things to Himself at the proper time.[16]

For Irenaeus, the overall consistency of God's actions in the economy is rooted in his triune being; we might say, his acts flow from his eternal character. For our purposes, the crucial consistency is found in the linking of creation, incarnation, cross and eschatology. The one through whom the world is created is the one through whom it was, is being and will be redeemed. The Word 'mingled with His own creation . . . suffered for us . . .' and 'will come again in the glory of His Father, to raise up all flesh . . .'

Let us explore some of the rich possibilities of this remarkable passage. (1) 'Mingled with his own creation.' Once again, we find that it is christology that provides an essential basis for a theology of character and virtue. The modern notion that to be human is to be a series of actions, decisions, choices – the ideology of the consumer society – is to take people out of the created matrix in which they are embedded. As the incarnation shows, this matrix has two aspects, the material and the social. The eternal Son of God became flesh – whole, embodied, human being; and he became flesh as one tied up with the social and political being of Israel, his people. Correspondingly, (a) Coleridge's moral slavery was also a bodily slavery to opium. This is but an extreme example of what we all are. As our willed actions become habitual, they correspond to

---

[16] Irenaeus, *Against the Heresies*, 3. 16. 6. This ought surely to dispel all the nonsense that Irenaeus's is only an economic trinitarianism, and that the evil of ontology came in only with Nicene theology.

tracks formed in the brain's nervous system, because our bodies embed what we are.[17] The incarnation of the eternal Son of God in Jesus of Nazareth establishes the necessity and possibility of the reorientation of the whole person. That in turn involves the development of proper perfections, virtues, correspondingly a renewal of the whole person, body, mind and spirit, a retraining of body as well as soul. (b) The social dimension involves similar claims. My disinclination to certain types of action and my tendency to perform others are functions of the way I was brought up and am still formed in both family and church, the way I was and am taught, the books I read and the way – to cite but one 'secular' example – the ubiquitous pressures of the modern media reinforce some and alter others of my – genetically and otherwise – inherited tendencies to act. All in all, to be a created human being is to be part of a material and social dynamic, and, because under the conditions of fallenness that dynamic is at once progressive and regressive, ecclesial formation exists to reorientate us to the eschatological promise of perfection in Christ; but it does so in a context which continues to resist it – hence 'at once justified and a sinner'. Therefore, every action makes for life or makes for death, and it is so not just for individual agents, but for the whole context, material and social, in which we live.[18]

(2) 'Suffered for us.' At this stage, we return to Ellen Charry's thesis that good theology is aretegenic, productive of virtue. In certain respects, this is a variation on Karl Barth's belief that dogmatics is ethics and ethics is dogmatics, but by specifically tuning into the recent rediscovery of the ethic of virtue, she enables the thesis to become more concrete than it sometimes appears to be in Barth. We have seen, however, that an ethic of virtue is not enough because character formation takes place in a dynamic of death as well as of life, so that vices need more than a process of retraining. Apart from redemption – in other words, apart from a radical redirection of the created order through Christ – death will have the last word. The fathers are

---

[17] That is not, of course, to adopt a crude mind-brain identity theory and conclude that brain states are identical with their actions, but to suppose that we are what we are in and as the particular bodies that we are.

[18] In sum: the modern understanding of autonomy cannot encompass a satisfactory account of created being, let alone of sin.

insistent that it is the corruption of the image of God in the human creature that is the source of the creation's subjection to vanity, to that nothingness which is the subversion of the creator's purpose. Accordingly, the Church cannot become a school of virtue unless she is first a community that lives and proclaims the forgiveness of sins achieved by the life and particularly the death of Jesus Christ her Lord as the sole basis of the reconstitution of the disabled human will. In traditional terms, justification is the precondition of sanctification. We cannot set out on the Hauerwasian journey without being turned about from the way we were going.[19] Anything else simply fails to do justice to the seriousness of the Fall in which all participate apart from redemption. There has to be a re-forming before there can be a forming. Things being what they are, characters are *de*formed: their settled disposition works against their eschatological perfecting rather than for it. In sum, we cannot use Jesus' formation in virtue simply as an analogy for ours. For, though he was like us in all things sin apart, that 'sin apart' presents a disanalogy so great that another, intermediate, step must be taken to supplement the weaknesses of an anthropology which is too Aristotelian.

With respect to the more explicitly churchly dimensions of our subject, it should be stressed that a theology of virtue must be grounded in a theology of baptism. Here the efforts of the self-consciously Anabaptist end of the free-church spectrum – and here I am making a general point, and not necessarily referring to Hauerwas directly – encouraged as its representatives are by Barth's theology of baptism, can militate against an ethic of grace. Joining, or being joined to, the Church is not an ethical act but one whose stress is on that which is received: the turning round of the old Adam symbolised by the water which drowns. The strengths of the traditions of infant baptism are that they stress that the path of virtue is one on which we have to be set, by others, as they place us in a community oriented to the death of Christ, a death which was, though finally chosen and after much struggle, imposed upon him by his Father. Only after going through that strait and narrow gate may we borrow – and

[19] As much of Hauerwas's theology makes clear. At issue is the matter of weighting: where the stresses are put.

therefore radically transform – the terminology of the worthy
Aristotle.

(3) We come now to the third feature of the passage from
Irenaeus: 'will come again in the glory of His Father, to raise up
all flesh . . .'; to which should be prefaced the conclusion of the
cited passage: that, 'as well as constituting Himself Head of
the Church, He might draw all things to Himself at the proper
time.' Irenaeus generates an eschatological ecclesiology,
without which we shall not find the anthropology we are
seeking. As 'head of the Church' Christ draws all things to
himself, 'at the proper time'. Any theology of virtue must take
shape within the fields of ecclesiology and eschatology. As
the community of the last days living before the last days,
the community of God's people exists to receive, through the
action of the Spirit, a forward orientation, away from the realm
of sin and death. The following few remarks will not attempt a
comprehensive account, but offer, I hope, at least a possibility
for further thought about this complex matter.

In Aristotle, as is often pointed out, there is a tension
between two conceptions of the purpose of virtue. First of all, it
is needed for the life of the polis; in that respect, clearly social.
But, second, human virtues exist to serve individual well-being,
eudaemonia, so that their *ethical* end is the pure contemplation
of thought thinking itself. They are thus secondary to a
theological end, individualistically conceived. Ethics in the
sense of a concern for the goodness and badness of human
action are not autonomous(!) but instrumental, a means to the
end that is contemplation of the timeless self-thinking thought
that is God. For Christian theology, ethics are similarly provisional, but not, I think, in so radical a sense as for Aristotle. We
are, according to the Letter to the Ephesians (2.10), created in
Jesus Christ for good works, and the incarnation necessarily
means that those things done in the body are of more ultimate
importance than they could be for either Plato or Aristotle. The
end, the purpose of it all, which Irenaeus has picked up at least
in part from this same letter, is that God in Christ may reconcile
all things to himself. The end is not contemplation of the
timeless but God's eschatological purposes for the whole
project of creation. One of the central means to that end,
signalled by the doctrine of the image of God, is the 'good

works' for which we are both created and redeemed. What is the place of the virtues in all this? How central do we make them?

IV   *The Church as a community of virtue?*

A recent writer has argued that the weakness of an ethic of virtue is that, unless its Aristotelianism is transcended, it contains a danger of ethical narcissism inasmuch as the subject's intentionality is directed towards itself and its own self-realisation.[20] Unless virtues come unnoticed and unremarked, they are not truly describable as virtues. It is in this light that the author brings to bear some criticisms by Luther of the Aristotelianism of both Aristotle and Aquinas as involving, in its tendency to narcissism, a problematic anthropology. It sees the human being too much as looking inwards, too little as oriented without. Against this, Professor Asheim shows that Luther's anthropology is *exzentrisch, enklitisch und responsorisch.*[21] In other words, virtue is received before it is exercised and takes shape in relation to what, with a change of meaning, we may call significant others.

There are two focuses for the exocentricity we need. First, the outward centredness has to be understood christologically and trinitarianly, moving from Jesus' human formation to that of others. Jesus' formation as the particular human being that he was is characterisable as a triune act: the incarnation – the sharing by God the Son in the human condition – can, as the work of the Son, only be understood as at once *also* the work of Father and Spirit. According to Hebrews the shape of this life was also fully human, for: Jesus was 'tempted in every way, just as we are – yet was without sin' (4.15), and that can surely serve as a summary of one side of the whole New Testament portrayal of the Saviour. Hebrews is emphatic: 'for this reason he had to be made like his brothers in every way, in order that he might

---

[20] Ivar Asheim, 'Lutherische Tugendethik', *Neue Zeitschrift für Systematische Theologie und Religionsphilosophie* 40 (1998), 239–60. As has often been pointed out, narcissism is another way of characterising the slavery in which modern Western society is bound.

[21] Asheim, 'Lutherische Tugendethik', pp. 245f.

become a merciful and faithful high priest. ... Because he himself suffered when he was tempted, he is able to help those who are being tempted' (2.17–18).

That latter reference to those who are tempted enables us to move by analogy to the condition of those for whom Jesus is the primary significant other. That members of the Church are forgiven sinners means that they enter the community, by baptism, with a common inheritance, that of fallen humankind. In genetics-speak, our genes encode bad information, which each of us embodies differently. Whatever some theologies of justification and some charismatic accounts of conversion may sometimes suggest, this bad information cannot be simply wiped from the slate. That would represent an over-realised eschatology. Although the 'bond which stood against us is cancelled' (Col. 2.14), God no longer counting our sins against us (2 Cor. 5.19), it is clear that the work of re-formation has only just begun. Whatever it may mean to say that 'you have been raised with Christ', the injunction, to 'seek the things that are above' (Col. 3.1) makes it clear that there is an end to be striven for. Paul's image of athletic training likewise indicates that the end in view both has to be worked at and is eschatological in character (1 Cor. 9.24–27).[22]

We can put this in the language we took from the Letter to the Hebrews. If Christ's perfect sacrifice offered to God through the eternal Spirit is the way for others to enter the sanctuary cleansed of their stain, then, to transfer to a combination of modish and Pauline language, training in virtue is *part* of the process consequent upon that sacrifice. But it is *only* a part. Romans 12.1–2, which flows from a theology of justification and election, combines sacrificial and ethical language: 'offer your bodies as a living sacrifice . . .'. The end – end as aim, *telos* – is not moral perfection, which is too narrow a concept, but virtues, human perfections, in the service of holiness, which is the offering of the whole person to God. Human virtue provides one of the central ways by which God the Spirit may enable anticipations of the end to be realised in course of the

---

[22] Thus we become virtuous not by imitating God – though there is an element of imitation – but by being brought into and maintained in a particular relation to God the Father through the Son and by the Spirit.

human journey, because it refers to the way settled dispositions to 'good works' are shaped. The fruits of the Spirit in the Apostle's list include forms of human being and action that are recognisably virtues: 'love, joy, peace, patience, kindness, goodness, faithfulness ...' (Gal. 5.22–23). These do overlap with the virtues of the Aristotelian philosopher, as forms of being human which enable a belonging with the other, but take significantly different shape because they serve to make human being truly an image of the being of the triune God.[23] In sum, it is the christological orientation which turns the moral agent outwards, away from self-development, to being conformed to the image of God which is Jesus Christ.

Christology is, then, the determinative motor of the exocentricity which take us from an Aristotelian to a biblical focus. There are two aspects. The first is that what can be called the channel of an exocentric theology of virtue is the worship and praise of God, grounded in faith. The heart of worship, and consequently also of training in virtue, is the actualisation of a relation to God the Father, mediated through God the Son by God the Holy Spirit. Worship is like the virtues in being a human practice learned from others, and only over a long process of time. It can serve the cause of virtue, but it is not itself the exercise of virtue, and is the primary activity of the Christian Church to which all other practices should be ordered. It is also a communal form of activity, however individualistically it is sometimes understood. Like the moral goodness with which we are concerned, it can come only as a gift, a gift which is an anticipation of the worship of the last times. Yet it is, as Paul's ever illuminating discussion of the Lord's Supper in 1 Corinthians 11 demonstrates, bound up with the moral shaping of the community. Those who respect economic and social divisions fail to recognise and practise the reality of the Supper; correlatively, the proper practice of worship bears fruit in transformed human relations. This, says Asheim, is Luther's view of the matter also. Those who are conformed to Christ's

---

[23] The contrast with Aristotle and his successors is also shown by the fact that we are here concerned not with the flight of the alone to the alone, but with the orientation of the community of faith to the promised Kingdom of God.

image are ground and pressed along with the wine and bread into a common form: the body of Christ, a fellowship of service which nourishes the world with its love, the blessing of the supper carrying over into an ethic.[24]

And that brings us to the second aspect of exocentricity, that virtues are not for self-realisation, but for the sake of the world. The Fourth Gospel teaches that the love within the community is to serve – its ulterior motive – the divine purpose of bringing all nations into the fold. This gospel's interest is primarily in the relation of the believing community to its Lord, but in view of the fact that other New Testament writings, and indeed John himself, teach that the one who became incarnate is the mediator of all creation, Irenaeus was not wrong to see in the use of bread and wine a promise of the participation of all created beings in the recapitulation achieved by Christ. A theology of ecological virtue can, with care, also be elicited from all this, but it would be wrong to make it anything but secondary to the primary values of human community. The whole world is represented in the bread and wine, but they are primarily a focus for the relation of human beings to their creator. The Holy Spirit's eschatological work is first of all focused on the personal, the renewed human community.

V   *Conclusion*

Finally, a return to the question of freedom with which the chapter began. First of all, we have learned, to be free is to be set free, and that is the point of the references to the cruci-fixion and baptism. They are free whom the Son liberates, as John 8.32–36 claims emphatically and repeatedly. But Christianity is not a fatalism or determinism which leaves things there, even though it has sometimes been made to appear like that. Freedom may need to be given, but it is given to be exercised, and can be defined even in individual terms as what we make of our human particularity. That of it which we receive as inheritance we are not free to change, in the sense that we

---

[24] Asheim, 'Lutherische Tugendethik', p. 251.

are at any time that which we have become. The gospel of forgiveness is rather that which gives resources – resources of the Spirit who perfects – for the movement of what we have been and are towards that which we shall be, when we are presented in Christ *teleios* before the throne of grace. They are free who are freed by the Spirit to praise God in both liturgy and life.

This orienting of freedom to the vertical realm, to God's action, has implications for the horizontal realm also. The freedom we must exercise is, on the one hand, what we receive from the others who contribute to the constitution of our persons; on the other, it is what we likewise give to others. That of course is why the families and other institutions intermediate between the individual and the State to which we belong are so important, and why their decline is so depressing a feature of the modern world. What, distinctively, of the Church? If we are not to make historically and morally implausible claims about the Church as a community of character and focus for training in virtue, we must define the Church exocentrically also, after Calvin, by reference to the primacy of the Word and sacraments. No moralistic criterion will do, because of the place of the incarnation, cross and resurrection. The Church is distinctively the institution that it is by virtue of its orientation to the Word and sacraments, the two constitutive features of its worship. According to the ecclesiology of the Fourth Gospel, the Spirit is the one who enables believers to share Jesus' relation to his Father, by incorporating us into it. That relation should not be understood, as it often is, experientially or individualistically – that is, as if individuals in some way replicated Jesus' relationship – but in terms of reconciled personal relations mediated within the structures of a community. These relations begin – anti-autonomously, we might say – by the acknowledgement of a headship ('we are not our own'); but lead to a form of autonomy, according to which the created *telos* of the human being – created for community with God and with others – comes to be, in anticipation of the community of the last days, from time to time realised. The virtues, therefore, are prominent, but not supreme, among the vehicles of human perfecting, and are not to be despised wherever and in whomsoever they are found. To grow in grace is to develop virtues, provisional perfections, and those settled dispositions are the matrixes for forms of human action which enable us to be that which we were created to be.[25]

---

[25] Particular kinds of persons tend to perform particular kinds of actions. Which comes first, the person or the act? If we are created for good works, then it would seem that the act is in the centre. Yet we both learn to be particular kinds of persons by doing particular kinds of acts, and in turn express what we have learned in further acts. That is the nature of the human person, somewhere between creation and perfection – or reprobation, as must, humanly, remain a possibility. The question is how we are to move between the one and the other, and the Christian account of the matter is that we are, by the converting and sanctifying Spirit, related first to God through Christ and then, at the same time, to one another. I am grateful to members of the Research Institute in Systematic Theology, and in this case especially Brian Brock, for helping me to work through these questions.

CHAPTER 7

ASPECTS OF SALVATION
Some Unscholastic Themes from Calvin's *Institutes*[1]

I *Calvin and context*

In approaching a text, particularly one called classic, a writer cannot escape his own expectations, which in this case means a general prejudice in favour of the view that where Calvin thinks trinitarianly – that is to say, with particular respect to the work of the Son and the Spirit mediating the act and will of God the Father – he is unequalled; when not, he is often deeply problematic.[2] Bound up with this are undoubtedly also the preoccupations of current scholarly discussion, for, particularly with respect to the doctrine of salvation, the debate about whether, and in what respect, Calvin taught that Christ died for all rather than for the elect is inextricably dependent upon his christology and pneumatology. Inevitably, that debate will colour the way in which Calvin is interpreted.

A second preliminary point takes us a little further. There is, without doubt, a difference of atmosphere between Calvin's *Institutes* and the doctrinal programmes before and after him, labelled in both cases, 'scholastic'. It has in large measure to do with two related features: its attitude to Scripture and its attitude to system. The scholastic temptation, mediaeval and

---

[1] Commissioned for an edition of the *International Journal of Systematic Theology* devoted to the consideration of classical theological texts, 1 (1999), 253–65.

[2] I am not making quite the same point as Philip Walker Butin, *Revelation, Redemption and Response. Calvin's Trinitarian Understanding of the Divine-Human Relationship* (New York: Oxford University Press, 1995), although the book is important in charting the importance of the Trinity in the structuring of Calvin's theology.

Reformed alike – often resisted, to be sure – is to use Scripture as a quarry for information that can be organised intellectually. Nowhere is this better illustrated than in the problems that arose in connection with Calvinist treatments of the doctrine of salvation. Here we need only allude to the disputes between Kendall and his critics. Whatever the criticisms of Kendall's scholarship, and Paul Helm has shown that in certain respects there are things to be found in Calvin which support more of a continuity than Kendall allows, there is a change.[3] I began by calling this a change of atmosphere. The challenge is now to be more specific.

One charge against the Reformed scholastics is the change from a covenantal to a contractual view of the relation between God and man.[4] Simply so stated, this misses the point. A contract is not in itself objectionable, nor a covenant necessarily benign. All depends on the nature of the relationship envisaged in each. Where there is more cause for alarm is in the move to a contrast between a covenant of works and one of grace. The systematic problem that it generates concerns the nature of Christ's substitutionary death with especial reference to the relation between Jesus and his Father. The change that was involved is well brought out in D. A. Weir's study of *The Origins of the Federal Theology*. 'Whereas John Calvin ... spoke of an Old Covenant which extended from after the Fall to Christ and then of a New Covenant which extended from Christ to the Day of Judgement, the Westminster Confession of Faith, written eighty years later, spoke of a covenant of works and a covenant of grace.'[5] The crucial difference – literally crucial – is that on the latter account it becomes easier to suppose that Christ as a man endures the punishment for the failure of Adam to maintain the covenant of works, and accordingly more difficult to construe the unity of the two Testaments that Calvin was so insistent on maintaining. In the one case, the work of the Son

---

[3] R. T. Kendall, *Calvin and English Calvinism to 1649* (2nd edn., Carlisle: Paternoster, 1997). Paul Helm, *Calvin and the Calvinists* (Edinburgh: Banner of Truth Trust, 1982).

[4] J. B. Torrance, 'The Contribution of McLeod Campbell to Scottish Theology', *Scottish Journal of Theology* 26 (1973), 295–311.

[5] D. A. Weir, *The Origins of the Federal Theology* (Oxford: Clarendon Press, 1990), p. 1.

and the work of the Father risk being torn apart; in the other, the Son's suffering is seen as a function of the love of the Father rather than of his punitive justice. Not that there are no punitive elements in Calvin; it is in any case difficult to contend that there are none in Scripture. But in some way that we shall have to explore the offence that there must be in any genuine theology of the cross is located in the wrong place by the federal scheme.

The key to Calvin's literary approach is in this context well expressed by Michael Weinrich:

> It was not dogma, the more or less orthodox church doctrine with its to some extent fantastic speculations – here the Reformers had in view the logically formal scholasticism of the late Middle Ages which had reached the point of absurdity – that was the centre for the Reformation but the witness of the Bible, with its proximity to life, i.e., all its embarrassments and surprises, its living drama and the continual wrestling with the presence of God, its plurality and simultaneous focus on the wholly inscrutable God who guides history.[6]

What is significant about Calvin's treatment of salvation, and particularly the great biblical themes of judgement and sacrifice, is the way in which he calls upon a wide range of imagery and biblical quotation in what would now be called a multi-layered way. Calvin is concerned with doctrine and dogma, but not for its own sake. The *Institutio* is an introduction not to theology but to the Bible, and that makes a great deal of difference. Let us then try to hear what he is saying, cutting out as far as is possible the background noise of recent disputation.

II *Anselmian echoes: the christological centre*

The second book of the *Institutio* opens with a reprise, made concrete, of the general teaching of the interrelation of the knowledge of God and of self which opens the work as a whole.

---

[6] Michael Weinrich, 'On Being Reformed Christians: Reformed Tradition in the Context of Modernity', unpub., p. 5.

The self which Scripture reveals is of primeval, original dignity, as being created in the image of God, and yet at present deeply corrupted. While it may be right to understand the Reformation as a retrieval of the Augustinian doctrine of grace in the light of mediaeval semi-Pelagianism, Calvin gently corrects Augustine's doctrine of sin into a generally more satisfactory mode: sin is not 'sensual intemperance' but infidelity leading to ambition, pride and ingratitude.[7] But the scholastics come under greater censure than Augustine, because they fail to realise that this corruption, though not natural, achieves a 'derangement' of our nature which corrupts both the intellect and the will, the latter in particular being described, partly on the authority of Augustine, as enslaved (II. ii. 8).

All this, however is said in the interest of the corruption's being overcome by grace. Book II is entitled, after all, 'The Knowledge of God the Redeemer', and the point of the opening chapters is to show that the will needs to be recreated through the renewal of the heart – a characteristically Reformation theme – and the achievement of this through the incarnation, death, resurrection and ascension of Jesus dominates the final chapters of the book. Chapter vi, which sets the scene for the treatment of salvation, represents a return to classical patristic themes, in a mode not often encountered in scholastic treatments, concerned as they tend to be with the articulation of doctrines. Here the stress is on the fact that faith in God is faith in Christ, so that mediation is central. 'In this sense, Irenaeus writes that the Father, himself infinite, becomes finite in the Son, for he has accommodated himself to our little measure ...' (II. vi. 4). It is that actuality which Calvin wishes to stress: personal knowledge of God is actually given in Christ.

The mood may be different from scholasticism, but the content is continuous, at least in the sense that Anselm's soteriology clearly shapes that of Calvin. The two theologians share something of a common apprehension of the basis of the Christian life in the death of the incarnate Son. The incarnation is for both of them God's response to desperate human

---

[7] John Calvin, *Institutes of the Christian Religion*, edited by J. T. McNeill, translated and indexed by F. L. Battles, Library of Christian Classics (Philadelphia: Westminster Press, 1960), vols. 20 and 21, II. i. 4. Further references will appear in parenthesis in the main text.

need, a need that puts the sinner beyond human or angelic resource. Calvin's account of this differs chiefly in being less an appeal to rationality, more to direct biblical citation, with characteristic appeal to 1 Timothy 2.5 ('one mediator') and Hebrews 4.15 ('a high priest who has in every respect been tempted as we are', xii. 1). Similarly, the subtle shift of emphasis from the necessity of the incarnation (which Calvin denies) to its graciousness also represents a change of mood and atmosphere. The incarnation takes place not to satisfy God's honour, or for his need of a full complement of heaven,[8] but is of grace, to make 'the heirs of Gehenna, heirs of the heavenly Kingdom' (xii. 2).

The very next section introduces another Anselmian parallel. For Calvin, too, only one who is both God and man can achieve the work of salvation. Anselm's argument that the situation is such that only God can achieve satisfaction, while only man ought to,[9] is displaced by a more Pauline note: 'since neither as God alone could he feel death, nor as man alone could he overcome it, he coupled human nature with divine that to atone for sin he might submit the weakness of the one to death; and that, wrestling with death by the power of the other nature, he might win victory for us' (xii. 3). (I shall return in the final section to the problems raised by the rather Nestorian form of that sentence.)

While it is by no means the case that for Anselm everything hangs on the cross of Christ as the place where satisfaction is won, it must be conceded that the details of the human career of Jesus are not of great interest to him. Calvin's more direct orientation to Scripture entails that for him the narrative shape of the saving incarnation has far greater prominence. After two chapters detailing the doctrine of the incarnation and the resulting Chalcedonian conception of the person of Christ, Calvin turns his attention to the saving history. The development of the doctrine of the three offices of Christ as prophet, king and priest enables him to link the Saviour with his Old Testament predecessors and models, and to frame his treatment of the past historic cross within a theology of the

[8] Anselm of Canterbury, *Cur Deus Homo*, I. 16–18.
[9] Anselm, *Cur Deus Homo*, II. 6.

present and future lordship of the ascended Lord. 'The Father
has given all power to the Son that he may by the Son's hand
govern, nourish and sustain us ...' (xv. 5). The climax is
the priestly office, so important for this great expositor of the
Letter to the Hebrews: 'as a pure and stainless Mediator he is by
his holiness to reconcile us to God' (xv. 6). Only with this
ground prepared does Calvin essay what today would, in
English language theology at least, be called an account of the
atonement.

There are two desiderata, representing two poles of the topic,
for a satisfactory treatment of the doctrine of the atonement.
One is to retain overall systematic control while enabling the
variety and richness of the biblical presentations of the fact
of salvation to emerge. The way in which the images merge
and blend in passages like Romans 3.24f. – 'justification',
'redemption', a 'hilasterion through faith in his blood' (to
translate literally and in the order of words of the Greek) – and
Colossians 2.14–15 – 'having set aside the bond ... with its legal
demands ... He disarmed the principalities and powers ...' –
has to be preserved if the many-sided richness both of the cross
and of its meaning are to be conveyed. The second desideratum
is that the three systematic criteria of classical christology be
maintained in this related context: that we see that this is a
divine act and a genuinely human achievement within the
frame of a unified personal history. Theories of so-called penal
substitution offend particularly against the latter of these,
making it appear that the Father and the Son have different
ends in view. And yet they do draw upon an aspect of the
biblical story which is inescapable if we are to take the whole
seriously. When the man Jesus goes to the cross, he goes to fulfil
what he acknowledged by being baptised: that in some way he
goes with the whole of Israel, and, as the outcome shows, the
whole human race, under the judgement of God the Father.
Only that can give due weight to the foreboding and horror
with which the passion narratives are loaded, quite apart from
their interpretation in the New Testament as a whole.

Calvin's account is based on the structure of what he calls
'the so-called "Apostles' Creed", which passes at once in the
best order from the birth of Christ to his death and resurrection, wherein the whole of perfect salvation consists' (xvi. 5).

The elements of this are held together in a multi-levelled treatment which could be called in the best sense a balancing act, in that Calvin never takes his eye off his destination, which is to present rather than explain the many-sidedness of that which is the love of God become historically particular in an Israelite man. 'However much we have brought death upon ourselves, yet he has created us unto life. Thus he is moved by pure and freely given love of us to receive us into grace' (xvi. 3). The achievement of salvation is described in a manner in which there is no one theory but biblical metaphors jostle together to build up a cumulative picture of cleansing, acquittal and redemption.

With the Letter to the Hebrews again in mind, Calvin makes much of Christ's obedience, making appeal also to Philippians 2. Like Anselm before him, Calvin stresses the voluntariness of the sacrifice of his life, without which it would have been ineffective. But more important still is the fact that Jesus' obedience to death is a function of his love as much as of his obedience alone: 'And here was no common evidence of his incomparable love toward us: to wrestle with terrible fear, and amid those cruel torments to cast off all concern for himself that he might provide for us' (xvi. 5). But, and this is the key, Christ's work of obedience *derives from* God's love; it does not *establish* it. Calvin cites Augustine at length to make his point. 'For it is not after we were reconciled to him through the blood of his Son that he began to love us. Rather, he loved us before the world was created, that we also might be sons along with his only-begotten Son – before we became anything at all.'[10] It is this which prevents the emergence of crude substitutionary teaching, and provides the essential context for Calvin's treatment of the juridical elements of the atonement, which otherwise might appear to take the form of penal substitution as that doctrine developed under the impact of the federal theology. This note is reinforced as Calvin approaches the discussion of substitution in the final chapter of the book:

> [I]t is absurd to set Christ's merit against God's mercy. For it is a common rule that a thing subordinate to another is not

[10] Calvin, *Institutes*, II. xvi. 4, citing Augustine, *John's Gospel*, cx. 8.

in conflict with it. For this reason, nothing hinders us from asserting that men are freely justified by God's mercy alone, and at the same time that Christ's merit, subordinate to God's mercy, also intervenes on our behalf ... 'God so loved the world ...' We see how God's love holds first place, as the highest cause or origin ... (xvii. 1–2)

The fact that Calvin so insists on the priority of God's love may, to the sceptically inclined, suggest that he has something to excuse or conceal. The more likely explanation, however, is that the note is often overlooked by those who look back at the Reformer through eyes given by later developments and fail to see how integral it is to his case.

Whatever we make of that, the fact remains that reconciliation on the biblical understanding requires an exchange, and that exchange is centred on the death of Christ, which accordingly involves that suffering is endured for and in the place of those who have merited it. To express this substitution Calvin uses a range of language, including both the juridical and the sacrificial, which, as in Paul and other New Testament writers, cannot finally be disentangled from each other. We have seen already that Jesus' action is described in sacrificial terms, as self-giving. It becomes for Calvin the vehicle of cleansing: 'The Son of God, utterly clean of all fault, nevertheless took upon himself the shame and reproach of our iniquities, and in return clothed us with his purity' (xvi. 6). The notion of blood, which is patient of interpretation in terms of juridical exaction, is, however, clearly linked with life and self-giving, as it is to the language of redemption. The following passage must be read as a whole if the breadth of Calvin's treatment is to be appreciated:

> For we could not believe with assurance that Christ is our redemption, ransom and propitiation unless he had been a sacrificial victim. Blood is accordingly mentioned wherever Scripture discusses the mode of redemption. Yet Christ's shed blood served, not only as a satisfaction, but also as a laver to wash away our corruption. (xvi. 6)

The substitution is real, and indeed penal, though not in the sense often understood; it is more in line with the Pauline teaching that Christ became a curse for us (Gal. 3.13, a text to which Calvin makes frequent appeal). Calvin indeed appears in the following passage to reject certain understandings of substitution:

> Yet we must not understand that he fell under a curse that overwhelmed him; rather – in taking the curse upon himself – he crushed, broke, and scattered its whole force. Hence faith apprehends an acquittal in the condemnation of Christ, a blessing in his curse. (xvi. 6)

Was ever more determined attempt made to take seriously the substitutionary character of the death of Christ without succumbing to a merely juridical or mathematical construal, what Irving was later to scorn as 'stock-exchange divinity'? Crucial is the fact that this is at once a divine and a truly human act: Jesus acts as both God and man. I continue the above citation from xvii. 2:

> We see how God's love holds first place, as the highest cause or origin; how faith in Christ follows this as the second and proximate cause. Suppose someone takes exception that Christ is only a formal cause. He then diminishes Christ's power more than the words just quoted bear out. For if we attain righteousness by a faith that reposes in him, we ought to seek the matter of our salvation in him.[11]

Here the note of mediation through Christ and his cross is central, and represents the continuing trinitarian construal of the atonement. It is also important to note that the crucified is for Calvin victor as well as victim, to use J. S. Whale's characterisation of two sides of the process.[12] 'For how could he by dying have freed us from death if he had himself succumbed to death? How could he have acquired victory for us if he had failed in the struggle?' (xvi. 13).[13]

---

[11] It may be that van Buren is right to point to the passages in which Calvin, rather Nestorianly, attributes the suffering of the cross to the humanity of Christ alone. Yet that is a christological point, and does not, I believe, detract from the soteriological claim that what happens here is the act of the divine Son who was there incarnate. Paul van Buren, *Christ in Our Place. The Substitutionary Character of Calvin's Doctrine of Reconciliation* (Edinburgh: Oliver & Boyd, 1957), p. 38.

[12] J. S. Whale, *Victor and Victim* (Cambridge: Cambridge University Press, 1960).

[13] Here Calvin in many ways parallels Athanasius's treatment of the atonement in *On the Incarnation of the Word*.

That quotation and its context reveal two things about Calvin's theology, its systematic richness – the refusal to do what is sometimes done, and reduce all to a single theory – and its interpretation of the cross only in the light of the resurrection, indeed of the whole story. Citing Romans 4.25 – 'He was put to death for our sins and raised for our justification' – Calvin prefaces the cited passage with the following words: 'This is as if he [Paul] had said, "Sin was taken away by his death; righteousness was revived and restored by his resurrection".' (xvi. 13). We can, moreover, in a later passage find Calvin building on this an account of the bearing of the ascension on the life of the believer. Again, he is able to use three of his earlier themes to develop a rich characterisation of the situation. First, there is the outcome of Christ's obedience: 'Since he entered heaven in our flesh, as if in our name, it follows, as the apostle says, that in a sense we already "sit with God in the heavenly places with him".' If we wish to apply a possibly restrictive label, we are here concerned with representation. Second there is the outcome of the substitutionary death: 'he appears before the Father's face as our constant advocate and intercessor. Thus he turns the Father's eyes to his own righteousness to avert his gaze from our sins ... He fills with grace and kindness the throne that for miserable sinners would otherwise have been filled with dread.' And, third, the outcome, in a move to a more military analogy, is the consequence of Christ's conquest of evil, that death is, and will be, swallowed up in victory. 'Thirdly, faith comprehends his might, in which reposes our strength, power, wealth, and glorying against hell' (xvi. 16).

If there has been in this account a note of defensiveness, it is because a careful reading of Calvin's treatment of the atonement makes it manifestly worthy of defence. Predisposed, if not predestined(!), by both the enthusiasm with which some later Calvinists have contemplated the fate of others in the toils of hell and the proper correction that Barth has attempted of his own Calvinist tradition, we so easily miss the sheer generosity of the picture of salvation painted so richly by this passionate and sometimes intemperate Frenchman. Without doubt he did limit its benefits to an elect minority whose restrictive definition falsifies the generosity of Scripture's God. But in that he did no more and no less than almost every

Western theologian before him. It is, therefore, appropriate to end this section with some words that effectively represent the pastoral character of Calvin's essentially non-scholastic theology:

> Hence arises a wonderful consolation: that we perceive judgment to be in the hands of him who has already destined us to share with him the honour of judging! Far indeed is he from mounting his judgment seat to condemn us! How could our most merciful Ruler destroy his own people? How could the Head scatter his own members? ... No mean assurance, this – that we shall be brought before no other judgment seat than that of our Redeemer, to whom we must look for salvation! (xvi. 18)

But we end with a puzzle, or at least what seems to this reader to be an unsatisfied promise. Summarising the significance of the crucifixion, Calvin comments: 'From this came that transmutation of nature (*illa naturae rerum conversio*)' (xvi. 6). What can that mean? It must in some way summarise the theme of the section, the bearing away of human sin and stain on the cross. It would appear to imply that the *exchange* has achieved some truly ontological *change*, a point that is not spelled out further. We may perhaps learn something of what is meant as we move to an exploration of some of the aspects of the appropriation of Christ's merits by believers, for that is undoubtedly the ontology with which Calvin is concerned.

III *Justification relativised? The mediation of the Spirit*

We preface this section with two preliminary points. The first is that it is sometimes remarked that Calvin, the impassioned and sometimes vituperative controversialist, never writes in criticism of Luther. That there are dogmatic differences which have shaped confessional differences ever since is, however, beyond dispute. A change in the order and the weighting of dogmatic loci effects ever greater changes the wider its impact is felt, and what we find in Calvin is not only a correction of the Lutheran stress on justification which can throw out of kilter other things that need to be said, but also a change of emphasis which introduces a major reorientation. The organisation of both Books II and III can be understood to defend the Reformation rearguard against attack, and some appreciation of what is happening is crucial to an understanding of what Calvin means by salvation.

Second, it must be observed that nowhere is there greater difference between the Reformers and their mediaeval predecessors than in their account of the appropriation of salvation. For Anselm, it scarcely features. This is, to be sure, largely for a reason rarely appreciated by his commentators, that his great book is not a treatise on the atonement but one designed to defend two features of Christian belief in salvation, its rationality and its eschatological purpose.[14] Yet the additional consideration must be taken into account that for a mediaeval the appropriation of salvation is simply given along with the Church and its sacraments and discipline. It just was not a problem for an early mediaeval monk. Once the mediaeval framework had been called into question, and particularly as radically as by that late mediaeval monk Luther, a whole new raft of questions required answering. It is time we heard less of the silly and individualistic characterisation of the Reformation as concerned with the question of how I can find a gracious God. The dispute was essentially ecclesiological, of how the grace of God is communicated in and through the Church. What is different – from Anselm, again – is that baptismal regeneration and the sacramental and penitential system of the Church is replaced by an act of grace to which the believer cannot contribute, but must respond. There remains in Calvin a theology of Christ's merits; but their benefits are conferred through faith, not baptism. This necessarily involved some attention to the particular believer, because already the cracks in Christendom were to be discerned, and the ground being laid for Kierkegaard's radical distinction between 'official religion' and Christianity. But let us return to Calvin, and particularly his third book.

We approach it by reconsidering an aspect of the second. Having introduced the book with a treatment of sin and the

---

[14] Anselm, *Cur Deus Homo*, Preface.

need for redemption, the Reformer had launched into an extended treatment first of the law – in general and as concentrated in the Decalogue – and then of the relation between the Testaments (II. vii–xi). This is the first of his attempts to ward off the more obvious of the attacks on the Reformation. If, he might be supposed to say, it is suspected that the Reformation is antinomian, this will disabuse its critics. The law has three uses, and prominent among them is the third use, the law as a guide for the Christian life. Calvin knows that the question of the law and the question of the unity of the canon are mutually involving. The gospel does not operate in a vacuum, but clears a space in which people may live.[15] The Old Testament knows this well. 'I understand by the word "law" not only the Ten Commandments, which set forth a godly and righteous rule of living, but the form of religion handed down by God through Moses' (vii. 1). Accordingly, Psalm 119 and the like, 'do not contradict Paul's statements' – which serve to make a different point – 'but proclaims the great usefulness of the law: the Lord instructs by their reading of it those whom he inwardly instils with a readiness to obey' (vii. 12). There is to be no rash rejection of Moses who, 'has admirably taught that the law ... ought among the saints to have a better and more excellent use', for: 'the law points out the goal toward which throughout life we are to strive' (vii. 13).

Calvin's strategy in Book III is similarly brilliant, heading off charges of antinomianism by opening the discussion of the appropriation of the gospel by a treatment of sanctification. In the order of the chapters there is to be seen a parallel with Calvin's treatment of sin and the law in Book II. Just as the actuality of the human fall and the goodness of God's provision of the law introduce the theology of salvation, so here the actuality of life in the Spirit is the first to be treated.

> Yet since we see that not all indiscriminately embrace that communion with Christ which is offered through the gospel, reason itself teaches us to climb higher and to examine into the secret energy of the Spirit, by which we come to enjoy Christ and all his benefits. (III. i. 1)

---

[15] I owe this point to Martin Wendte.

Crucial here is Calvin's avoidance of any suggestion that faith is a work rather than being the gift and instrument of the Holy Spirit. It is here that attacks on scholastic intellectualism preface a characteristically Reformation emphasis on the heart. Calvin's definition of faith perfectly illustrates the point made above, that when he structures his thought trinitarianly, no one is better. Faith is 'a firm and certain knowledge of God's benevolence toward us, founded upon the truth of the freely given promise in Christ, both revealed to our minds and sealed upon our hearts through the Holy Spirit' (ii. 7). The knowledge of the heart is both more difficult and more central than the merely intellectual: 'It is harder for the heart to be furnished with assurance than for the mind to be endowed with thought. The Spirit accordingly serves as a seal, to seal up in our hearts those very promises the certainty of which he has previously impressed upon our minds ...' (ii. 36). Once again, pneumatology is central, as it is in the characteristically polemical discussions which follow of penitence and confession, contradistinguished as they are from penance and satisfactions, and their implied doctrines of indulgences and purgatory.[16] Once again, as in the previous Book, Calvin wards off suggestions of antinomianism. Commenting on biblical passages which imply God's seriousness about breaches of the law, he comments that 'if these passages mean that vengeance shall be repaid – which is beyond doubt – we must also not doubt that by contrary statements the Lord affirms that he remits all penalty of vengeance' (iv. 29).

These are long chapters, concerned as they are both to attack the intellectualism and Pelagianism of the scholastics and to guard himself from falling into the contrary errors. After them, Calvin moves to somewhat shorter chapters on the Christian life, which, again, is stressed as a matter of the heart. These chapters are clearly designed as an enrichment of the earlier

---

[16] These discussions illustrate the fact that Calvin is at once a traditionalist and a humanist. Both appear in *Institutes* III. iv. 39, the latter in his scholarly rejection of forged pastiche, the former in his appeal to the Fathers against the scholastics: 'in the present argument almost all [Lombard's] evidence is taken from Augustine's book *On Repentance*, which was bunglingly patched together from good and bad authors indiscriminately.'

exposition of the law,[17] and their theme is self-denial, the taking up of the cross, 'contempt' for the present life without hatred of it. Here there is an attempt to present the law without legalism: not to define such precise laws so as to bind consciences too tightly by forbidding enjoyment, but to show that the law does matter.

There are thus ten chapters before Calvin comes to justification, with the appropriation of salvation being treated before an account of its reception. It is not that justification has not already shaped Calvin's treatment of the Christian life. As we have seen, the attacks on indulgences in particular depend upon it, and its presence is felt in the treatment of faith from the very beginning. 'For in God faith seeks life: a life that is not found in commandments or declarations of penalties, but in the promise of mercy, and only in a freely given promise' (ii. 29). The treatment is again trinitarianly structured and rooted in a conception of present participation in Christ:

> By partaking of him, we principally receive a double grace: namely, that being reconciled to God through Christ's blamelessness, we may have in heaven instead of a Judge a gracious Father; and secondly, that sanctified by Christ's spirit we may cultivate blamelessness and purity of life. (xi. 1)

Calvin's cumulative definition of justification in xi. 2 insists that it lies in a relation to God, not in some legal fiction: Therefore, we explain justification simply as the acceptance with which God receives us into his favour as righteous ... And we say that it consists in the remission of sins and the imputation of Christ's righteousness. Legal fiction perhaps not, but it is the juridical metaphors which, hardly surprisingly in view of the concept we are exploring, dominate the treatment of justification. Yet they are metaphors: acquittal means not simply remission of penalty, but personal acceptance, and, indeed, good works as consequence – works, indeed, which gain their value from God's approval rather than from their intrinsic value (xi. 20).

---

[17] 'The law of God contains in itself that newness by which his image can be restored in us. But because our slowness needs many goads and helps, it will be profitable to assemble ... a pattern for the conduct of life in order that those who heartily repent may not err in their zeal', *Institutes*, III. vi. 1.

Participation is again the key: justification derives from the atonement achieved by Christ (xi. 9), but more especially from participation in the risen and ascended Christ himself: 'our righteousness is not in us but in Christ, that we possess it only because we are partakers in Christ' (xi. 23). To Luther's austere alien righteousness is added a participatory note which dominates this whole book. Calvin can even sometimes speak of a 'mystical union' with Christ (xi. 10).

Calvin believes that justification by faith can be shown to be necessary for almost every theological and pastoral reason that can be imagined. What he does not do with it, as generations after him did try to do, was to turn it into a theory, or into part of a theory, of an *ordo salutis*. That, again, was the way of scholasticism, and it is not his way. That is not to say that he is uninterested in practice; quite the reverse. But the treatment remains theocentric in a way rarely matched by Calvin's successors. Pastorally, it is the only teaching that at once frees the conscience (xiii. 3) – so generating good works – and protects from complacency and arrogance; theologically, it is necessary at once for God's glory and for the fulfilment of his promises, promises fulfilled in his mercy to sinners (xii. 7). Accordingly, it at once meets the deepest needs of the fallen and reconciled human being and demonstrates the justice of God. In short, it is the doctrine by which the Church stands or falls.

IV   *Qualifications*

The foregoing and largely celebratory account of the work of this great theologian should not be taken to imply that there are no warts on the face of the one of whom Barth memorably said that it was 'Religion ... which laid upon Calvin's face that look which he bore at the end of his life.'[18] It is, however, difficult to identify precisely what form they take. The best way of making the general point is that there is in Calvin an undertow which always threatens, but never succeeds – perhaps

[18] Karl Barth, *The Epistle to the Romans*, translated by E. C. Hoskyns (London: Oxford University Press, 1933), p. 259.

the problem with 'Calvinism' is that there it more nearly did succeed – in drawing the ship on to the rocks. Various attempts have been made to identify it, perhaps most memorably in Barth's repeated wish that Calvin had taken more seriously his belief that God is indeed as he is made known in Christ. As Barth's pupil, Paul van Buren, puts it in this very context, 'Calvin clearly is holding back, reserving, as it were, some other characteristics of God that apparently are not revealed in Christ'.[19] For him, the symptom is that Calvin separates the suffering of the human nature of Christ from that of the divine.[20] That may be right, but whether Barth's attempted correction in his parallel account of the doctrine of substitution-representation in the *Church Dogmatics* is finally any more satisfactory must remain in question. The danger here is that the suffering of God displace, or, perhaps more judiciously put, tend to overshadow the human work of Jesus of Nazareth. Calvin's treatment of the human priesthood of Christ seems to me manifestly more satisfactory than that of Barth.

Yet a problem remains, and, as has been suggested from the outset, it is trinitarian. In this realm, there are two ways of diverging from the straight and narrow. They are represented on the one side by Calvin's tendency to separate the divine and human reality of the one Christ and on the other by Barth's to assimilate the two. Trinitarianly, two features must be maintained: that the Son does indeed do the Father's work, so that (1) to know him is truly to know the Father; and yet (2) not in such a way that his work is indistinguishable from that of God the Father. The Father sends, and the Son obeys, not merely as God obeying God,[21] but as the incarnate and fully human Jesus obeying, in the power of the Spirit, the will of the one who sent him. The heart of the doctrine of substitution is not God as God *simpliciter* standing in his own dock, as in the truly memorable treatment by Barth,[22] but God the Son bearing as man the weight of the Father's holy wrath against sin.[23]

---

[19] van Buren, *Christ in Our Place*, p. 12.

[20] van Buren, *Christ in Our Place*, pp. 12, 22.

[21] As Jüngel has memorably shown to be Barth's teaching, unsurprisingly appealing to his Lutheran commentator. Eberhard Jüngel, *Gottes Sein ist im Werden* (Tübingen: J. C. B. Mohr (Paul Siebeck), 2nd ed., 1967), p. 100.

[22] Karl Barth, *Church Dogmatics*, translation edited by G. W. Bromiley and T. F. Torrance (Edinburgh: T. & T. Clark, 1957–1975), §59.2, 4/1, pp. 211–83.

[23] Readers may hear an echo of P. T. Forsyth in this formulation.

One inch from that path, and we are in the objectionable realms of either penal substitution or a mere exemplarism. But the dangerous path must be trodden, for unless we tread it, as Calvin did, we shall fail to articulate either the depth of the human plight or the divine and human cost of our redemption.

CHAPTER 8

ELECTION AND ECCLESIOLOGY IN THE POST-CONSTANTINIAN CHURCH[1]

I *The problem*

It is often enough averred that Calvin developed his doctrine of predestination in order to reassure believers of their status before God; it is even more often asserted that the overall effect of his teaching was eventually to subvert that assurance, or at any rate to turn it into a form of self-absorption that has an effect contrary to that for which the gospel frees us. Self-absorption is indeed among the besetting sins of Western Christianity, from Augustine onward. In each era, it takes characteristic form. In our day, it is among the prime dangers of the post-Constantinian Church, which, deprived, apparently, of once secure social and political status and role; diminished, apparently, in numbers and influence, flounders variously in inaction, activism and political correctness in a sometimes desperate concern not to lose the attention of the – reprobate? In this chapter, I propose to bring together the related themes of election and ecclesiology, with particular reference to the beleaguered situation of the Christian Church in a world which, as Robert Jenson has observed, is unique in being the first once apparently believing culture to have abandoned the Christian gospel. That throws into the limelight the problem of the, if not everywhere minority status, at least

[1] Written for a conference on the Reformed Theological Tradition organised by the Center of Theological Inquiry, Princeton, in Heidelberg, March 1999. First published in *Scottish Journal of Theology*, 53 (2000), 212–27.

unique situation for the Church of rejection by the main streams of intellectual and cultural life.

Augustine and Calvin were right in one thing: the elect are indeed a minority. That, surely, is the message of much of the New Testament, as also of Luther's suggestion of making persecution one of the marks of the Church.[2] This is the case, however, not because the mass of perdition is going to hell, though, of course, it may be; but, I would contend, because God elects the particular in order to achieve his universal purposes. Here, the doctrine of election, properly stated, should serve the cause of a due ecclesial self-confidence, one based not in individual assurance of future salvation, though that may be an integral part of it, but in a call to ecclesial faithfulness. That is the proposal to be explored in this chapter, because in it lies the basis of a genuinely universal contribution to the Church's calling that may be made on the basis of Reformed teaching.

II   *Election and ecclesiology*

Another oft-repeated truism is that the work of the magisterial Reformers still operated within an essentially Constantinian model of the relation of Church and State, by which I mean, quite neutrally, a social arrangement according to which it is assumed that in certain respects Church and State or Church and society will be coterminous. Over against this, the thesis to be argued is that the development of the theology of dissent in England offers interesting possibilities for an ecclesiology which is yet free from the Pelagianising tendencies which seem sometimes to mark the ecclesiologies of the so-called radical Reformation. The dissenting stream of the Reformed tradition offers models of a stronger distinction-in-relatedness between the Church and its social context than did Constantinianism, without falling into the voluntarist theologies of baptism and church membership which mark both Barth and modern Anabaptism alike.

[2] I owe this point to Ian McFarland, *Listening to the Least. Doing Theology from the Outside in* (Cleveland: Pilgrim Press, 1998), p. 70.

Part of the resolution of the problem is to be found in the doctrine of election. Theologies of election have tended to suffer from two questionable formulations, both rooted in the same weakness. After Barth, indeed, after Arminianism, we are all too aware of the weakness of the traditional Augustinian-Calvinist form of the teaching. Under what has come to be called Constantinianism its tendency is to conceive the elect and the reprobate as two classes *within* the Church, with the true, invisible, Church being known only to God. In reaction to it, a form of voluntarism tends to develop, an Arminianism stressing the free adherence of the believer and easily degenerating into a form of self-election. Barth's teaching serves as a corrective. All people are, at least *de jure*, among the elect, because they are already contained within the corporate Christ by virtue of his eternal election to be the one he is in the becoming/being of the triune God.[3] It is scarcely fair to say that it was in order to compensate for the apparently universalist implications of this doctrine that Barth introduced his theology of baptism, but that is none the less the effect that it has in the overall weighting of his dogmatics. To counterbalance a determinist-seeming theology of election there is introduced a theology of the sacraments which over-determines the human act, under-determines the divine.

The common weakness of the two formulations is to overweight the protological and underweight the eschatological determinants of the doctrine of election. Or rather: eschatology is so determined by protology that the end is effectively determined by the beginning, and history is, apparently, closed to the recreating work of the Spirit. To justify this thesis requires a brief and no doubt tendentious historical recitation. Augustine's view of creation as a timeless and instantaneous willing of the whole of time and space makes something like the double decree inevitable, unless he is to follow the universalist path of Origen. As we know, he does not, yet Origen's contribution is essential, for it shapes the form that Western eschatology later takes. Significant here is first his insistence

---

[3] Karl Barth, *Church Dogmatics,* translation edited by G. W. Bromiley and T. F. Torrance (Edinburgh: T. & T. Clark, 1957–1975), 2/2, especially perhaps, §33.

that God creates a *finite* number of immaterial spirits, whose pre-mundane fall requires the creation of the material world to provide a period of (re-?)training in human bodies;[4] and second the (almost) entirely other-worldly eschatology that is its consequence. Under the impact of a pre-temporal creation of a non-material being, eschatology inevitably comes to mean the return of the spirits to the pure immateriality of the beginning.[5]

Once that picture is in turn modified by Augustine's pessimistic and this-worldly view of the origin of sin, the problem of the finitude of the complement of heaven becomes acute. Eschatology continues to be other-worldly, but its outcome is the teaching that the end of creation, the eschatological purpose of God, is to fill the complement of heaven with a finite number of the saved. The seriousness with which Anselm enquires at length whether the number of the saved will equal the number of fallen angels is in this respect Western theology's most revealing passage.[6] The foreordained complement of heaven requires to be made up, the outcome being that the new heaven and the new earth of biblical promise give way before a view that God foreordains a limited number of the elect to complete an essentially other-worldly aim. Although there were always counter-influences, so long as the doctrine of the resurrection of the body continued to be confessed and taught, Anselm's formulation reminds us that there is little that is materially new in Calvin's doctrine of predestination, at least so far as the number and destiny of the elect are concerned. What is materially new, and it was to be developed further by Barth, is the greater orientation to Israel and Christ.[7] What later became historically new is the

---

[4] Origen, *De Principiis*, II. xi. 6; vi. 3.

[5] J. W. Trigg, *Origen. The Bible and Philosophy in the Third-century Church* (Atlanta: John Knox, 1983), p. 110.

[6] Anselm of Canterbury, *Cur Deus Homo*, I. 16–18. Notice the Origenist aspects of the following, with its essential aesthetic construal: 'We cannot doubt that the rational nature, which either is or is going to be blessed in the contemplation of God, was foreseen by God as existing in a particular reasonable and perfect number, so that its number cannot fittingly be greater or smaller' (*Cur Deus Homo*, I. 16).

[7] John Calvin, *Institutes of the Christian Religion*, edited by J. T. McNeill, translated and indexed by F. L. Battles, Library of Christian Classics, vols. 20 and 21 (Philadelphia: Westminster Press, 1960), III. xxi–xxii.

way the doctrine of predestination came to dominate theological controversy to such an extent that revulsion has made it almost impossible to mention the doctrine without misunderstanding.[8]

However, there are moments of truth in the received doctrine, and we must affirm on biblical grounds that election is indeed prevenient and particular. Some, and therefore presumably not others, are chosen, apart from their willing and in advance of their acceptance. 'The Lord did not set his affection on you and choose you because you were more numerous than other peoples ... But it was because the Lord loved you and kept the oath he sware to your forefathers ...' (Deut. 7.7–8). So it is also with the election of particular people within Israel, including especially kings and prophets. 'Before I formed you in the womb I knew you, before you were born I set you apart ...' (Jer. 1.5). Notice that Jeremiah is, on this account, created in order that he might be a prophet to Israel. We should bear in mind here Scripture's insistence that Israel's call is not only prevenient and unmerited but also irrevocable. 'God did not reject his people, whom he foreknew' (Rom. 11.2) and, as that chapter of Paul's shows, the same is the case with those within Israel who remain true when all others have become apostate: 'I have reserved for myself seven thousand who have not bowed the knee to Baal ...' (Rom. 11.4, citing 1 Kings 19.18). Writing to a church which contains both Jew and Gentile, the apostle sets her election in what must be called pre-eternity: 'For he chose us before the foundation of the world to be holy and blameless in his sight. In love he predestined us to be adopted ...' (Eph. 1.4).

The most pressing systematic problem, engaged in another context by Augustine (far more rigorously, it must be said, than some of his critics) is in this context that of the relation of time and eternity. If God is the creator of time, then necessarily his acts will be 'from without', and, it would seem, election 'from before'. Barth similarly sees that election is at once an eternal and temporal act, and the greatness of his treatment is

---

[8] I once preached on election in King's College Chapel, and one of the more intelligent of the listeners needed to see a copy of the script before she could be convinced that I had not propounded eternal and predestined reprobation.

its interlocking, interweaving, of eternal and historical divine act. However, in systematic theology balance and weighting are, if not everything, undoubtedly crucial. Here, as chaos theory suggests, a minor shift in initial conditions can have immense implications for the remainder of a system, and it is character-istic of the sensitivity of Barth's dogmatic antennae that he gives in advance indications of the weakness of his proposal and hints as to where a solution might be found. Those theologies, he says, which fail to give due weight alike to the pre-temporality, supra-temporality and post-temporality of God fail to incor-porate the overall thrust of the Christian gospel.[9] What then is the place of post-temporality in Barth's treatment of election? The crucial shift that we have already met in the history of this doctrine is Origen's, with his spiritualising eschatology, and its reverberations are still to be felt in Barth, albeit weakly.[10] What tends to disappear from view is the kind of eschatology to be found in Scripture, for example in Ephesians, Romans 8–11 and the Apocalypse. Relevant features are: a greater orientation to the destiny of this material creation as the context which is also inextricably bound up with the goal of the human; a conse-quently different conception of the way in which eschatology might be conceived to be realised; and, in sum, a more concrete pneumatology.

What might this threefold cord contribute? Let us begin with one of the most important contributions of Calvin to theology, his affirmation of the unity of the Testaments and therefore of the divine economy.[11] Taken seriously, and with a stress on the promise of the resurrection displacing his tendency to prefer the dangerously ambiguous 'immortality', this would involve greater attention to the historical calling of Israel construed as something more than the people from whom the Christ was born. Whatever the precise meaning of the promise to Abraham in Genesis, its meaning for Paul is clear. The

[9] Barth, *Church Dogmatics* 2/1, pp. 615–20.

[10] Douglas B. Farrow, *Ascension and Ecclesia. On the Significance of the Doctrine of the Ascension for Ecclesiology and Christian Cosmology* (Edinburgh: T. & T. Clark, 1999), pp. 241–54.

[11] 'The covenant made with all the patriarchs is so much like ours in substance and reality that the two are actually one and the same. Yet they differ in the mode of dispensation.' Calvin, *Institutes*, II. 10. 2.

descendants of Abraham were, are and remain elect, and their rejection is not eternal like that of the Calvinists' reprobate, but temporary and instrumental. 'Israel has experienced a hardening in part until the full number of the Gentiles has come in. And so all Israel will be saved ...' (Rom. 11.25–26). The historical election of Israel is with a view to the election of representative Gentiles, after which it will be re-established and perfected. Noteworthy is (1) that we are here concerned with the election of communities, not individuals from within communities; and (2) that the realisation of eschatology takes place in time in advance of its completion in eternity.

By contrast, Augustine can indeed use Israel as a model, but his problematic takes him into rather different byways. As TeSelle points out,[12] 'infants can be saved only through baptism or its counterpart in Israel, circumcision and membership in the chosen people'. What are the problems here? Predominating are those deriving from an over-emphasis on the ultimate salvation of the individual. Barth is right that the doctrine of election goes astray when much weight is borne by analysis, on the basis of observation, of the fact that some believe and others do not.[13] But what he sees to be characteristic of Calvin, others have attributed to Augustine, as the father of this way of thinking. 'Predestination is viewed ... as the ultimate explanation of the actual – at least the *observable* – course of events.'[14] Bound up with this preoccupation with the faith and destiny of the individual, and distorted by it, are all those problems associated with a proper concern with attributing the gift of salvation to God. 'Augustine thinks that predestination involves *two* problems ... one of *the beginning of faith*, and another one of *perseverance to the end* ...'.[15]

As cannot be too often recalled in discussion of this question, election has to do with definiteness – with determinateness – and not with determinism. A Reformed, indeed I would want to say a biblical, account should be able to accept that both the beginning of faith and the capacity

---

[12] Eugene TeSelle, *Augustine the Theologian* (London: Burns and Oates, 1970), p. 323.
[13] Barth, *Church Dogmatics* 2/2, pp. 38–44.
[14] TeSelle, *Augustine*, p. 325.
[15] TeSelle, *Augustine*, pp. 324f.

to continue in it are the gifts of God. In the former, we cannot avoid an element of *pre*determining, *fore*ordaining. Otherwise, what can we make of the call of Israel and Jeremiah, let alone the first two chapters of the Gospel of Luke? The offence in the way the Augustinian tradition has construed it is clear: it lies in the fact that God's choice is rendered gratuitous rather than gracious, surely another casualty of the quantitative approach to the question of the complement of heaven that we have already met. The proper interest served by the doctrine of election concerns not the numbers, but the purpose of the election of such quantities as there are, paradigmatically for our age of ecclesial anxiety, perhaps, Elijah's seven thousand. It is that God's will should continue to be done in Israel and on earth. In other words, it is an ecclesial matter before it is concerned with the individual believer: with what Israel and the Church are here for rather than the fate of individuals within them.

It is in connection with the latter of the two dimensions of the life of faith – perseverance – that we are perhaps able to open the question a little. Do we not need to be able to say that this, too, is the gift of God, to a degree foreordained? And yet must that be taken to be the equivalent of absolutely pre-programmed? An answer to that will be approached by reference to another weakness of the traditional doctrine, where two disastrous shifts took place: away from an ecclesiology of *koinonia* – grace mediated communally – to one of inwardness; and away from a conception of the action of the eschatological Spirit enabling right human response to a conception of grace as a semi-substantial force either assisting or determining human perseverance *causally*.[16] (In the either/or is contained, in a nutshell, almost the whole Reformation debate, and, as TeSelle has pointed out, both conceptions ultimately derive from Augustine's attempt

---

[16] See Robert Jenson's remark about the tendency to identify the work of the Spirit as a process, as the means of God's causal action upon us, rather than, say, his free personal relation with us. Robert W. Jenson, 'The Holy Spirit', *Christian Dogmatics*, edited by C. E. Braaten and R. W. Jenson (Philadelphia: Fortress Press, 1984), vol. 2, pp. 126f.

to find room for human freedom in his doctrine of perseverance.)[17]

What is lost in all this is a theology of the eschatological Spirit enabling right human action within the Church and in anticipation of the final reconciliation of all things. If the Spirit is the electing God,[18] and if the Spirit is the one who gathers the Church to the Father through Christ in order that his will be done on earth, then somewhere in that vast dogmatic minefield are to be found clues to the way we should take. Here we must distinguish between the Spirit's universal creating work and the way by which he perfects creation by enabling particular events to realise eschatological truth and goodness in created time and space. The Spirit, 'in transfusing into all things his energy, and breathing into them essence, life, and movement ... is indeed plainly divine'.[19] The Spirit's creating work is, before it is anything else, universal. However, the point of the story of Israel's election and Jesus' resurrection is that the universal end of creation – 'to bring all things in heaven and on earth together under one head, even Christ' (Eph. 1.10) – is achieved through particularities.

Among those particularities, and indeed, pre-eminent among them, are Israel as the people of God, and the Church

---

[17] 'Augustine states repeatedly that the gift of perseverance is a grace that "cooperates" with men ...' TeSelle, *Augustine*, p. 328. He appears to have bequeathed to the tradition two possibilities, inherent as both were in the ambiguities of his thinking about grace and freedom. The first is what became Calvinist double predestination, and we need not linger with it, except to say that it is preferable to its alternative. For some of the reasons why almost anything is preferable to 'Arminianism', see Robert W. Jenson, *America's Theologian. An Appreciation of Jonathan Edwards* (New York: Oxford University Press, 1988). The second is a development of a doctrine of co-operating grace, which muddied the waters and still muddies them, as is shown by recent debate about the *Joint Declaration on Justification*. All such doctrines generate a doctrine of divine-human interrelation in which the human and the divine are in some way in co-operation or competition. The doctrine of grace displaces that of the Spirit, according to which human action does not co-operate with the divine because it is *enabled by it*. Only thus can action be seen to be authentically human without in some way appearing either to compete with, co-operate with or be overridden by divine action.

[18] 'The speaking of the gospel is the event of predestination in that the gospel gives what it speaks about, but this eschatological efficacy of the gospel is the Spirit. We must parody Barth: the Holy Spirit is the choosing God.' Jenson, 'The Holy Spirit', p. 138.

[19] Calvin, *Institutes* I. 13. 14.

as the body of Christ. The election and calling of the *particular*
communities is rooted in the universal mediation of creation in
Jesus Christ. The relation between creation, its eschatological
perfecting and the place of the Church in it is perfectly
expressed in the words of another Pauline letter. 'He is before
all things and in him all things hold together. And he is the
head of the body, the church ... so that in everything he might
have supremacy ...' (Col. 1.17, 18). Once again, the passage
brings together heaven and earth in its eschatological promise:
'to reconcile to himself all things, whether things on earth or
things in heaven, by making peace through his blood ...' (v.
20). On such an account, the elect are not primarily those
chosen for a unique destiny out of the whole; rather, they are
chosen out of the whole as the community with whom the
destiny of the whole is in some way bound up. It follows that
what is needed to correct imbalances in historic treatments of
our doctrine is a stronger orientation to the bearing of post-
temporality on the present than either Calvin or even Barth was
able to achieve.

III   *Election and the post-Constantinian Church*

It is at this stage that we can introduce the contribution of the
generations after Calvin, particularly in England, shaped as it is
by their greater involvement in discussion of the Church's
being over against Constantinian forms of Christianity. John
Owen is, on the face of it, the last person we should expect to
be of assistance. As Cromwell's chaplain, he is hardly a post-
Constantinian figure; as proponent of a scheme of 'federal
theology' at odds with Calvin's stress on the unity of the
covenant, his dual predestination often sees him placed in
the class of those rigid Calvinists who are alleged to have
distorted the master's theology. Yet he has contributions to
make which can, taken apart from his doctrine of limited
atonement, generate an approach to election which is more
christological and pneumatological, and therefore more
historical and eschatological than that of the tradition.

The first is that although Owen is not, in the modern sense,
a voluntarist, he insists on the incompatibility of the gospel

with any manner of coercion. ('Is there no means of instruction in the New Testament established, but a prison and a halter?')[20] This enables the formulation of a *theology* of toleration – and thus of the relation of Church and the social order – which need owe nothing to the individualistic rights theory of liberal modernity. Appealing to a pre-Constantinian tradition, he points out that, 'For three hundred years the church had no assistance from any magistrate against heretics.... As the disease is spiritual, so was the remedy ... and the Lord Jesus Christ made it effectual'.[21] There is also to be heard a note of eschatological reserve which enables the Church to combine confident acceptance of election with a relatively open stance to those not elect, or apparently not so.[22] That is to say, there is in this theologian of double predestination an essentially christological defence of toleration, and therefore the basis of an ecclesiology which is both Reformed, appropriately confident and 'modern', even allowing for 'pluralism' of a kind.

Second, and in a related way, Owen's christology enables greater attention to be given to the humanity of Christ as the locus of divine action and election; that is to say, to concentrate attention not on a pre-temporal election, in either Calvinist or Barthian form, but on election as the genuinely historical realisation of, indeed, God's actual eternal purpose, which is not the salvation of a few but something manifested in the fact that 'the Gentiles are heirs together with Israel ...' (Eph. 3.1–11). What is interesting is that Owen's Christ is indeed the eternal Son become flesh, but also the chosen one whose life is at once predestined by God the Father and enabled and realised by the action of God the Holy Spirit. The Spirit is the one who, as Jesus' inseparable other, relates him to

[20] John Owen, 'Of Toleration', *Works*, edited by W. H. Goold (Edinburgh: T. & T. Clark, 1862), vol. 8, pp. 163–206, p. 171.

[21] Owen, 'Of Toleration', p. 183.

[22] In dispute with Rome's over-realised eschatology, represented by Bellarmine, Owen points out that according to 1 Cor. 11.19 'heresies' are 'for the manifesting of those that are approved, not the destroying of those that are not...' Quoting 2 Tim. 2.25, 'Waiting with all patience upon them that oppose themselves, if at any time God will give them repentance ...', Owen comments: 'Imprisoning, banishing, slaying, is scarcely a patient waiting', p. 202.

the Father and so enables his response which is both obedient and free.[23]

This has important anthropological and soteriological impli-cations. What the Spirit performs in relation to the humanity of Christ, he can be seen also to do in relation to those who are the adopted – elect – brothers and sisters of the risen Jesus; that is to say, enable them to realise their freedom. This is an escha-tological act, for it involves liberating *from* the chains of sin *to* the maturity of the children of God. It is also eschatological in that it will be perfectly realised only at the resurrection, although from time to time that realisation is anticipated through the Spirit's agency. Systematically, this provides a means of developing a more open doctrine of election than those to which reference has been made in this chapter, including Barth's. Only the Spirit can reconcile lost human beings to God the Father through Christ – by election – yet the Spirit's otherness, modelled on the New Testament depiction of his relation to Jesus, generates an openness according to which the Spirit can determine that relation through an election which is yet uncompelled because it is the means of the realisation of the sinner's true being in Christ. The function of the otherness of the Spirit is thus to confirm and re-establish the true otherness of the creation in reconciled relation to God. In that way, the Spirit crowds out grace as a semi-hypostatic reality intermediate between God and the world.

It is in the words 'in Christ' that we find the heart of the matter of the right relation of electing God and temporal world. In contrast to both Augustine and Barth it has to be taken more temporally in terms of election to the worship and life of a concrete earthly people gathered out of the peoples of the world. In other words, a stronger reference to the actual historic community is needed in place of both Augustine's otherworldly individualism and Barth's heavenly-earthly Christ. The latter is right to see election as being 'in Christ' but more questionable when he tends to see the whole human race as *immediately* in Christ rather than *mediately*, as Israel and the

---

[23] 'The Holy Ghost . . . is the *immediate, peculiar, efficient cause* of all external divine operations . . .' Owen, *A Discourse Concerning the Holy Spirit, Works*, vol. 3, pp. 160f. See Alan Spence, 'Inspiration and Incarnation: John Owen and the Coherence of Christology', *King's Theological Review* XII (1989), 52–5.

Church historically elected by the Spirit's eschatological enabling.

We now reach our third contribution from Owen, which consists in the fact that this predestinarian theologian is able to be surprisingly 'voluntarist' in his doctrine of the Church. Given that the Church is the particular number of the elect gathered in Christ by the action of the eschatological Spirit, we are now enabled to conceive their free action as voluntary although determined. For Owen the Church takes form through human acts of free obedience, but can only do so because it is elect. 'Wherefore *the formal cause of a church* consisteth in an obedi-ential act of believers ... jointly giving themselves up unto the Lord Jesus Christ, to do and observe ...' [24] What else is that obedience but response to an election to be in a particular form of relation to others, as the examples of Israel, Jeremiah and Jesus in different ways indicate?

If, however, this account is not to run the risk of appearing to reduce election to vocation, the shape of divine action in relation to those called into the Church requires further speci-fication. Here three dogmatic focuses will enable this to take place. The first is contributed by Robert Jenson, in Lutheran mode: 'Predestination is simply the doctrine of justification stated in the active voice. If we change "We are justified by God alone" from passive to active we get "God alone justifies us"'.[25] Election therefore becomes for Jenson the other side of justifi-cation and so part of his polemic against modern Arminianism, the peculiarly but by no means solely American teaching that we elect ourselves. 'It is a strict corollary of the Reformation doctrine of justification: All things happen by God's will.' [26]

We shall return to the problem raised by that final assertion, but not before there has been some discussion of the means by which predestination is realised. It is sometimes charged against Calvin that he sees the Church and the sacraments as the contingent rather than intrinsic means by which the purposes of God are realised. (Book IV is after all entitled: 'The external means or aims by which God invites us into the society

---

[24] John Owen, *The True Nature of a Gospel Church, Works*, vol. 16, pp. 11–208, p. 29.
[25] Jenson, 'The Holy Spirit', p. 134.
[26] Jenson, 'The Holy Spirit', p. 135.

of Christ and holds us therein'.) The orientation I have been attempting, of placing greater weight on the actual historical election of Israel and the Church, acts as a counterweight to the danger of divorcing the gospel from the Church. If election is first of all *revealed* as and through the election of Israel and the Church, can such a suspicion remain? Here, supplementing Jenson's stress on justification a second dogmatic notion, that of incorporation, provides a more explicitly christological focus. 'Those God foreknew he also predestined to be conformed to the likeness of his Son ...' (Rom. 8.29). On this account, election is not merely vocation, because it entails also being made part of the body of Christ, incorporate in him who died and was raised. This means that election for the Gentile consists in being made in some way to share Israel's election, and that partly for the sake of Israel herself. Paul makes this clear in Romans 11, where an image he uses (vv. 17–22) is the horticultural one of engrafting. Gentiles are a branch grafted on to an already existing root stock. This in turn entails a relation of near identification: if the Church is the body of Christ, those incorporate by baptism are more than merely called. There is an ontological change, because they have entered a new set of relationships, with God, with other people and with the created order.

Third, the pneumatological dimensions of incorporation are in turn provided by the notion of adoption. It is almost a commonplace of Christian theology that only one is Son of God by right; others attain that status by the grace of adoption. Adoption is the Spirit's means of realising God's election of particular people into the body of Christ. This means again that election, for the Gentile, takes the form of being elected alongside Israel in part for the sake of Israel. The logic of this had been set out earlier in the same letter. '[T]hose who are led by the Spirit of God are the sons of God ... And by him we cry "Abba, Father". The Spirit himself testifies with our spirit that we are God's children' (Rom. 8.14–16). The Spirit brings particular human beings into actual and transformed relationship with God the Father, realising their election. The catena of Rom. 8.30 brings into view something of the point being here made, that far more should be made in this context of the concrete historical event of election. 'And those he predestined he also called; and those whom he called, he also justified; and those whom he justified, he also glorified' (Rom. 8.30).

And yet we cannot avoid here the implications of the Pauline 'foreknew'. Election is indeed rooted in eternity, because it is an act or acts of God. This means that from our point of view if it is to be grace, it must be prevenient, must come before the human act of obedient choice that is the due response to it. The case stands thus. Because God is eternal, his acts, as embracing time with eternity, cannot be placed on the same time-scale as ours, so that any naive attribution of them to past, present and future is excluded. However, that does not mean that care is not required in relating election to the time line on which we understand that we live, an understanding shaped by the temporal structure of the economy of salvation, of which election is a part. The need here is not to solve all the problems, or indeed any of the problems, of the logic of time and eternity, so much as to construe the relation of the different episodes in the economy of divine action in such a way that none is over- or underweighted so as to distort the biblical message. Here we can draw a parallel. If the notion of creation in the beginning is stressed at the expense of creation's eschatological direction and destiny, the latter can come to appear as no more than the outworking of a determinist scheme. If, similarly, as we have seen, the eschatology of the human is understood too transcendentally, too spiritualistically, too individualistically, the actual details of the biblical portrayal of election – that is to say, its historical outworking through Abraham, Israel, Jesus and the Church – become merely or mainly Platonic shadows of an eternal reality, not the concrete locus of God's saving action.

By contrast, the kind of eschatology envisaged here, with the resurrection conceived as the anticipation and beginning of an end that is neither this-worldly nor other-worldly, but in some sense the completion and transformation of this heaven and earth into a new heaven *and earth* – will give more weight than has hitherto been the custom to election's temporal outworking: in this case the *before* will not be stressed at the expense of the constitutive importance of what happens after the beginning and before the end. This does not even require that there can be no prelapsarian dimension to election; 'he chose us in

[Christ] before the creation of the world' (Eph. 1.4). Those willed to be chosen on this account are not primarily to be understood – though they may for all we know be that second-arily – as those who will end up in heaven, but those by whom God's universal purposes are to be mediated. That the purposes should be mediated by disobedient Israel and crucified Messiah is indeed contingent on the Fall; but it does not follow that Israel and the incarnation are not willed from eternity. The key, as the critique of the Augustinian doctrine of election was designed to suggest, is in the content we give variously to the *destination* and the *pre*, and the way we relate them. We shall not by this change of emphasis evacuate the gospel of offence, as the above quotation from Jenson will demonstrate.[27] What we shall do is remove the false offence, that because Israel and the Church are elect, it necessarily follows that all other human beings will end up on – at best – the rubbish heap of history.

In conclusion: despite the fact that the Reformed notion of obediential freedom came in time to be contaminated by secular and individualistic accounts of freedom, the ecclesio-logy of Dissent has much to teach us. If the Church is to be the Church in the post-Constantinian age, she must renew her sense of her (passively constituted) *calling* to be a particular people serving a universal end. 'Who will bring any charge against those whom God has chosen? It is God who justifies' (Rom. 8.33). Only by a turning away, enabled by the Lord who is the electing Spirit, from the self-absorption of those who have lost their sense of direction to an orientation to the promised reconciliation of all things in Christ can this happen.

IV   *Concluding apologetic postscript*

It was pointed out in discussion of the original presentation of this chapter that there is in such an approach a danger that something from the old conception of election may be lost: the joy in believing that belongs to those who know that they are among the elect.[28] It must be conceded that if an over-moralistic

---

[27] Referenced at note 26 above.
[28] I thank Steve Holmes for this point.

conception of the servant Church is the outcome, perhaps the move to a more historical conception of election is a mistake. But it need not be over-moralistic. The point about the dangers of Constantinianism does indicate a real flaw in the Church's historical witness, so that the change of social and political orientation need not entail a diminution of the doctrine's edifying effect on the life of the Church. There is here, in any case, no intention to deny the grounding of election in God's eternal will for his people nor any need to treat the two movements as alternatives. Why should not this election equally be a cause of rejoicing? So the point of the chapter remains: in this doctrine, so characteristic of the Reformed tradition, there is surely something we can with profit harvest unashamedly from our Reformed tradition.

CHAPTER 9

SOLI DEO GLORIA?

Divine Sovereignty and Christian Freedom in the 'Age of Autonomy'[1]

I *Identifying the problem (1): the glory of God*

Eric Heaton's Oxford lectures on the Old Testament prophets in the late 1960s indicated his manifest dislike of the concern of Ezekiel, that austere Barthian, with the glory of God's name and the apparent self-preoccupation of God which it evidenced. Yet similar expressions are not absent from many other books of the Old Testament canon. In view, therefore, of the grim harvest of the semi-Marcionism and covert anti-Semitism of so much of the Christian tradition, we ignore it at our peril.[2] We shall not develop an adequate Christian theology unless we can at least do justice to this side of the Bible's characterisation of the God of Israel, leading as it does to the work of Ezekiel's greatest disciple, the author of the Apocalypse. There we are reminded of the eschatological perfection of the divine glory and its christological mediation: 'The city does not need the sun or the moon to shine on it, for the glory of God gives it light, and the Lamb is its lamp' (Rev. 21.23). Nor should we forget – in the context of the Reformed tradition in particular – that one of Scripture's greatest ascriptions of glory to God is to be found in the completion of Paul's treatment in Romans 11 of the eschatological reconciliation of

---

[1] Written for a conference on 'The Future of Reformed Theology', Westminster College, Cambridge, September 1999.

[2] For part of the long story of Marcionism's modern influence, see Francis Watson, *Text and Truth. Redefining Biblical Theology* (Edinburgh: T. & T. Clark, 1997), especially chapter 4.

Jew and Gentile in obedience to the one God of them all –
perhaps the nearest Paul comes to universalism.

A second allusion to the Old Testament reinforces the point
learned from Ezekiel that the God of Scripture is not necessarily what we would call 'nice'. 'God behaves like the crabby old
cuss that we know Him to be': so the writer Jonathan Keates on
the God of the Books of Samuel.[3] If we are to be true to
Scripture, we may not forget that the God and Father of our
Lord Jesus Christ is the God of the Old Testament, and the God
of the Old Testament is not to be mocked. He has the first and
last word, even though he allows his friends, quintessentially
Abraham, Moses and Job, much scope for argument on the way.
Robert Jenson is right. If we look here, at the God of Israel, we
have a God among whose essential attributes is jealousy.[4] He
will not tolerate from Israel – from anyone, indeed – worship of
anyone or anything else. There is much competition in recent
theology among the candidates for what is the essence of sin,
whether it be pride, violence, or, as in some feminist ripostes to
this supposedly male preoccupation, a failure to value oneself
adequately. In their different ways these all tend, however,
when stated so baldly, to construe the matter non-relationally,
in terms of symptoms alone. Against this, there is a case for
saying that for Scripture all depends on the disrupted relation
to God, which is best understood in terms of idolatry, the
worship of gods, people – including and quintessentially
the self – or things, rather than and above their creator. In our
context, that must be construed to mean that sin is that human
attitude and action which gives glory to anything other than the
God of Scripture.

We should not, I believe, or not yet, construe this zeal for the
honour of God's name merely anthropocentrically, as though
God's jealousy of all rivals is primarily manifested in the human
interest: that is to say, God is jealous simply in order that we
should not display the symptoms which so radically disrupt our
life on earth. The God of Deuteronomy, of the prophets and

[3] Jonathan Keates, 'God's tales of blood and thunder', *The Spectator*, 30
January 1999.

[4] 'In the Scriptures ... it is first among the Lord's attributes that he is "a
jealous God".' Robert W. Jenson, *Systematic Theology*, vol. 1, *The Triune God* (New
York and Oxford: Oxford University Press, 1997), p. 47.

the psalmists – to take just some examples – is intrinsically jealous of any rival, intrinsically the one God who will tolerate no rival. Those who forget this, or attempt to live as if it were not so, simply deceive themselves. We should not therefore necessarily take offence when Calvin makes God's glory one of the reasons for his justification of the sinner. 'Do you see that the righteousness of God is not sufficiently set forth unless he alone is esteemed righteous, and communicate the free gift of righteousness to the undeserving? ... For, so long as man has anything to say in his own defence, he detracts somewhat from God's glory.'[5] (For Calvin, that is not the whole story, and the matter is held in dialectical relation with the outcome of such a stance, 'that our consciences in the presence of his judgement should have peaceful rest and serene tranquillity'; yet the dialectic is rightly not resolved into a claim that the divine glory is there for the sake of the peaceful conscience. It is to be celebrated for its intrinsic significance, because God is God.)

Yet it is also easy to turn our God into a devil. This has been the accusation sometimes levelled against the God of certain forms of predestinarian Calvinism – for example, that he is made to be in some way directly responsible for the Holocaust.[6] Does God glory in the death of the sinner? For some, so it would seem, as is instanced by the confident knowledge of some Calvinists that hell will not be empty: 'By the decree of God, for the manifestation of his glory, some men and angels are predestinated unto everlasting life, and others fore-ordained to everlasting death.'[7] Whatever we make of this, it is difficult to square with the eschatological visions of Romans 8 and Ephesians 1.[8] And yet, without conceding anything to

---

[5] John Calvin, *Institutes of the Christian Religion*, edited by J. T. McNeill, translated and indexed by F. L. Battles, Library of Christian Classics, vols. 20 and 21 (Philadelphia: Westminster Press, 1960), III. xiii. 1. I cannot forbear to cite his next sentence also: 'Thus in Ezekiel, God teaches how much we glorify his name by recognizing our iniquity.' Compare Barth's somewhat more affirmative statement: 'God's glory is God's love. It is the justification and sanctification of us sinners out of pure, irresistible grace.' Karl Barth, *Church Dogmatics*, translation edited by G. W. Bromiley and T. F. Torrance (Edinburgh: T. & T. Clark, 1957–1975), 2/1, p. 645.

[6] I do not see how we can avoid conceding that God is in some way indirectly responsible for the Holocaust, at least in the sense of permitting it.

[7] *Westminster Confession of Faith* (1646), III, iii.

[8] See chapter 8 above.

Westminster's prelapsarian ordination of personal creatures
to the cosmic bonfire, we cannot, on the basis of Scripture,
accept an axiomatic universalism either. As in all theology,
there is a fine line to be drawn somewhere, and here it is
between, on the one hand, turning God into a self-obsessed
tyrant, and, on the other, a liberal sentimentalism which refuses
to acknowledge that God's glory and the perfection of his
creation may involve acts and attitudes with which we are not
comfortable, including the eschatological violence to which
Miroslav Volf has so finely drawn attention:

> it takes the quiet of a suburban home for the birth of the
> thesis that human non-violence corresponds to God's refusal
> to judge. In a scorched land, soaked in the blood of the
> innocent, it will invariably die. And as one watches it die, one
> will do well to reflect about many other pleasant captivities of
> the liberal mind.[9]

Is modern suspicion of the affirmation that all things should
serve the glory of God, and specifically its taking shape in the
claim of the Westminster Shorter Catechism that 'the chief end
of man' is 'to glorify God and to enjoy him for ever', one of
those captivities? We shall return to the question, but first we
must explore the other pole of our topic.

II *Identifying the problem (2): the limitations of freedom according to the Reformed tradition*

Calvin's account of human moral and religious slavery is
directly in the tradition of Augustine and the Luther of *The
Bondage of the Will*. Yet the modern world represents the
triumph of Erasmus, in a form, however, that he is unlikely to
have relished. The situation, accordingly, is as follows: that in
aiming for human liberation in terms of liberation *from* God,
the modern world has constructed a prison for the spirit – I
allude to J. R. R. Tolkien's reply to the charge of escapism, that
if you are in jail, escape is scarcely to be refused – such that the
cure is worse than the disease. There are, to be sure, a number

---

[9] Miroslav Volf, *Exclusion and Embrace. A Theological Exploration of Identity,
Otherness, and Reconciliation* (Nashville: Abingdon Press, 1996), p. 304.

of sides to modern 'liberalism'. One of them is that its concern
for freedom surely echoes that of Scripture, and in its historical
origins might indeed be understood as a challenge to
Christians, in an age when the gospel appeared to have been
distorted into a tool of repression, to organise themselves
according to their own standards. We are, however, at present
experiencing the darker side of the matter, because if anything
is evident at the present time it is that the arrogation of
freedom has engendered the most frightful slaveries, whether
in the violent history of our century or in the disastrous social
and personal effects of the modern myth of self-realisation.

The questions are those of the meaning and source of
autonomy. What is the most proper law of our own being, and
how is it realised? At the extremes, we are faced with an
absolute contrariety: either our autonomy comes from God,
because he is the creator and redeemer from whom *all* dimensions of our being and action derive; or it comes from ourselves,
because anything else would be a violation of our personal
freedom. The doctrine of creation does indeed imply a *relative*
independence of God, and the doctrine of the image of God
implies that human being ought to have that distinctly personal
quality we call freedom. Yet neither implies that freedom is
outside the relation of the creature to its creator. Here,
the doctrine of sin complicates the matter, especially for the
Augustinian and Reformed tradition, because it implies
something about the radical incapacitation and corruption of
both human and non-human created reality: a – relative or
radical – loss of freedom in fact.

Let us review three classic analyses of human incapacity from
representatives of, and in the third case someone influenced
by, the Reformed tradition. Calvin's treatment of 'The
Knowledge of God the Redeemer in Christ' which is the second
book of his *Institutio* is introduced with an extended treatment
of that universal human bondage which is theologically
described as sin. In opposition to mediaeval semi-Pelagianism,
he contends that sin is an unavoidable derangement of that
which is natural. Of relevance for our enquiry is the fact that for
him it deprives human beings of freedom. The subtlety of
Calvin's discussion is remarkable, for in it he is able to do
justice at once to the depth of human bondage and to the

freedom of God the Holy Spirit to enable human science, art and political order despite the opposition.[10] The bondage is entered into freely, yet in such a way that freedom is lost. Calvin quotes Augustine's definitive analysis: 'Through freedom man came to be in sin, but the corruption which followed as punishment turned freedom into necessity.' The crucial distinction is between necessity and compulsion.

> Now when I say that the will bereft of freedom is of necessity either drawn or led into evil, it is a wonder if this seems a hard saying to anyone, since it has nothing incongruous or alien to the usage of holy men. But it offends those who know not how to distinguish between necessity and compulsion.

What is noteworthy is that this distinction is justified by a *theological* analogy which shows that necessity and freedom are conceivably compatible: 'from his boundless goodness comes God's inability to do evil. Therefore, if the fact that he must do good does not hinder God's free will in doing good ... who shall say that man therefore sins less willingly because he is subject to the necessity of sinning?'[11] Just as, we might say, God's necessary doing of the good is a function of his being what he is – of his ontology – so the human necessity to sin derives from the human condition of universal fallenness.

It is important to note here that Calvin does not deny the continuing reality of the will. Here his authorities are Augustine and Bernard, showing that the Reformed tradition is here in complete continuity with aspects of its patristic and mediaeval inheritance. 'For man, when he gave himself over to this necessity, was not deprived of will, but of soundness of will.' He cites Bernard's analysis at length:

> 'Among all living beings man alone is free; and yet, because sin has intervened he also undergoes a kind of violence, but of will, not of nature, so that not even thus is he deprived of his innate freedom. For what is voluntary is also free.' And a little later: 'In some base and strange way the will itself, changed for the worse by sin, makes a necessity for itself. Hence, neither does necessity, although it is of the will, avail

[10] Calvin, *Institutes*, II. ii. 12–17.
[11] Calvin, *Institutes*, II. iii. 5.

to excuse the will, nor does the will, although it is led astray, avail to exclude necessity. For this necessity is as it were voluntary.'[12]

We shall return to the relation of necessity and freedom, but must first engage with the Enlightenment's unsuccessful attempt to articulate it.

By the time of Jonathan Edwards, Enlightenment thinkers – of whom he was one, as we must always remember[13] – had subjected the Augustinian and Calvinist philosophy of the will to sustained, if, as Edwards was to show, naive analysis. His great treatise therefore enables us to enrich our picture of the human bondage which can be ended only by redemption. Edwards argues essentially that no willed act is without cause, so that to speak of absolute freedom, what he called freedom of indifference, is an absurdity. 'To suppose the will to act at all in a state of perfect indifference, either to determine itself, or to do anything else, is to assert that the mind chooses without choosing.'[14] For example, no consciously willed act is entered on without some motive, which thus operates *causally*.

But if every act of the will is excited by a motive, then that motive is the cause of the act of the will. If the acts of the will are excited by motives, then motives are the cause of their being excited; or, which is the same thing, the cause of their being put forth into act and existence. And if so, the existence of the acts of the will is properly the effect of their motives. Motives do nothing as motives or inducements, but by their influence; and so much as is done by their influence is the effect of them. For that is the notion of an effect, something that is brought to pass by the influence of another thing.[15]

[12] Calvin, *Institutes*, II. iii. 5, quoting Bernard, *Sermons on the Song of Songs* lxxxi. 7. 9.

[13] Robert Jenson, *America's Theologian. A Recommendation of Jonathan Edwards* (New York and Oxford: Oxford University Press, 1988).

[14] Jonathan Edwards, *A Careful and Strict Enquiry into the Modern Prevailing notions Of that Freedom of Will, which is Supposed to be Essential to Moral Agency, Vertue and Vice, Reward and Punishment, Praise and Blame*, edited by Paul Ramsey (New Haven and London: Yale University Press, 1957), p. 198.

[15] Edwards, *Freedom*, p. 225.

What Edwards demonstrates is that freedom is not the exercise of a will that is somehow other than the person as a whole. There is no 'inner person' or homunculus which is somehow a replica of the outer while being free (*sic*) from the outer's involvement in relations of influence and determination within the structures of worldly reality. The latter expression is perhaps a gloss or extension of the point Edwards is making about motivation, but it holds. Human beings are *creatures*: that is to say, beings whose reality is what it is by virtue of their interrelatedness in time and space with other creatures. The extent of the determination – whether it should be understood in terms of predestination or 'determinism' – is here not to the point. What is relevant is that for the creature, caught up in a web of 'influences', there simply is no undetermined act. If there is 'freedom' it must be understood within the terms of human creaturehood as it actually is, and the strength of Edwards' analysis is in part that it stands for the human condition in general, even had Adam not fallen.

At this stage we can pause to recall that Kant ('the century's coming to an understanding of itself – but of itself in its limitations'[16]) was aware enough of the problems involved to attempt to circumvent them. Unlike Edwards, however, he wishes to have his cake and eat it: to affirm determinism in a strong sense and an almost absolute freedom of will in parallel with it. His dialectic of inner moral freedom and outer determinism is an evasion of the problem, as later debate, even until today, has demonstrated beyond peradventure. Yet Kant's awareness of the age's limitations involved a contempt for a mere moral optimism which drove him deeper. His doctrine of radical evil ('Is it possible with impunity to be so far in agreement with St Paul as Kant after all was in his doctrine of sin?'[17]) laid the ground for an analysis not simply of the constitution of the will in its relationship with its creator and its situatedness in the web of creaturely existence, but of its bondage. This bore fruit in the nineteenth century in a

---

[16] Karl Barth, *Protestant Theology in the Nineteenth Century: Its Background and History*, translated by B. Cozens and J. Bowden (London: SCM Press, 1972), p. 266.
[17] Barth, *Protestant Theology*, p. 297.

deepening of the analysis of the psychological realities which underlie Calvin's dialectic of necessity and freedom.

Coleridge's account, aided as it was by both his engagement with Kant and his entrapment in addiction to drugs, enables us to penetrate further into the well-springs of the slavery that is sin. Before citing Coleridge's penetrating analysis, it is worth pausing to say how much we owe here to recent explorations of character, virtue and *habitus* which enable a realisation that we are who and what we *particularly* are in large measure as the result of the way in which we are both made and make ourselves by our moral formation and the acts which contribute to it; and that formation takes shape in a social nexus. While Schleiermacher's doctrine of sin in other respects can be argued to underestimate the depth of the human plight, he is perceptive on its social dimensions:

> Whether . . . we regard it as guilt and deed or rather as a spirit and a state, it is in either case common to all; not something that pertains severally to each individual and exists in relation to him by himself, but in each the work of all, and in all the work of each; and only in this corporate character, indeed, can it be properly and fully understood . . . [T]he aggregate power of the flesh in its conflict with the spirit . . . is intelligible only by reference to the totality of those sharing a common life . . .[18]

Schleiermacher's great contemporary knew something more profound still about both the guilt and the slavery which his sin involved, and his perceptiveness about the individual's condition advances our argument:

> By the long habit of the accursed Poison my Volition (by which I mean the faculty *instrumental* to the Will, and by which alone the Will can realise itself – its Hands, Legs & Feet, as it were) was completely deranged, at times frenzied, dissevered itself from the Will and became an independent faculty: so that I was perpetually in the state, in which you may have seen paralytic Persons, who attempting to push a step forward in one direction are violently forced round to

---

[18] F. D. E. Schleiermacher, *The Christian Faith*, translated by H. R. Mackintosh and J. S. Stewart (Edinburgh: T. & T. Clark, 1928), p. 288.

the opposite. I was sure that no ease, much less pleasure, would ensue: nay was certain of an accumulation of pain. But tho' there was no prospect, no gleam of Light before, an indefinite indescribable Terror as with a scourge of ever restless, ever coiling and uncoiling Serpents, drove me on from behind.[19]

The distinction between the will – that personal centre which we have seen Bernard and Calvin to maintain even after the Fall – and the volition – the will in operation – enables us to see something of the psychological shape of the bondage that is sin. Coleridge's radical reappropriation of the above cited saying of Calvin, 'For man, when he gave himself over to this necessity, was not deprived of will, but of soundness of will' may appear to characterise only the deeply wicked and addicted, and not be generalisable to the human situation as a whole. But two recent analyses of sin in relation to the modern evasion of the reality of universal human fallenness have reminded us that it is a difference of degree, not kind. Miroslav Volf's response to the travails of Croatia has demonstrated that in this conflict no one is free from at least a measure of guilt. The crisis is a demonstration of the lost human condition as a whole: 'A particular evil not only "inhabits" us so that we do what we hate (Romans 7.15); it has colonized us to such a thoroughgoing extent that there seems to be no moral space left within the self in which it could occur to us to hate what we want because it is evil.' [20] The language of colonisation is the language of enslavement by something that takes away autonomy, our proper being in the world. Similarly, one of the strengths of Cornelius Plantinga's recent *Breviary of Sin*[21] is that it shows that the modern arrogation of freedom is in fact a form of displacement, so that what we generally take to be freedom is in fact a radical form of slavery. When God is displaced by the human will, what eventuates is not freedom but all kinds of self- and other-destructive activity and attitudes. And the point does not apply

---

[19] Cited by Richard Holmes from S. T. Coleridge, *Letters* III, pp. 189–90, in *Coleridge. Darker Reflections* (London: HarperCollins, 1998), pp. 356f.

[20] Volf, *Exclusion and Embrace*, pp. 89f.

[21] Cornelius Plantinga, *Not the Way It's Supposed to Be. A Breviary of Sin* (Grand Rapids: Eerdmans, 1995).

simply to the social and psychological realms, but to our interaction with the broader environment. Our arrogation of
absolute freedom distorts our relation with the whole universe,
as Christoph Schwöbel's discussion of freedom in ecological
context demonstrates.

> In order to generate reliable policies of action the modern
> rhetoric of absolute freedom requires comprehensive
> knowledge of all these aspects of action. But, in fact, our
> knowledge is limited. It is not only quantitatively limited, but
> qualitatively limited in that it is mediated through our social
> forms of existence and the physical processes of our inter-
> action with our environment. The modern rhetoric of
> freedom persuades us to ignore these limitations of our
> action-directing knowledge systematically ...[22]

All these features of unfreedom masquerading as freedom can
only be understood theologically, in terms of that fundamental
disorientation of the human relation to God that is sin, and
quintessentially the sin of idolatry, for the attempted exercise of
absolute freedom is but a way of playing God. Edwards'
description of what he calls the Arminian conception of
freedom could be a description of God's: 'a self-determining
power in the understanding, free of all necessity; being
independent, undetermined by anything prior to its own acts
and determinations; and the more the understanding is thus
independent, and sovereign over its own determinations, the
more free.'[23] Edwards knew, without benefit of the destructive
realities which this conception has helped since his time to
generate, that it was simply mistaken, because it implied that
the less rational the agent is, the more free.[24]

---

[22] Christoph Schwöbel, 'Imago Libertatis', *God and Freedom: Essays in
Historical and Systematic Theology*, edited by Colin E. Gunton (Edinburgh: T. &
T. Clark, 1995), pp. 57–81, p. 66.

[23] Edwards, *Freedom*, p. 223. As we shall see, such a conception is not even to
be attributed to God.

[24] 'Certainly, 'tis no liberty that renders persons the proper subjects of
persuasive reasoning, arguments, expostulations, and suchlike moral means
and instruments ... [A]ccording to this, the more free men are, the less they
are under the government of such means, less subject to the power of evidence
and reason, and more independent of their influence ... ' Edwards, *Freedom*,
pp. 223f.

In many respects, to be sure, none of this is original. What gives it its power is the fact that a highly persuasive account of the modern doctrine of the freedom of indifference suggests that it is tantamount to the Augustinian-Reformed doctrine of sin. In turn, the plausibility of that is reconfirmed by the crisis of modern social and international order, if such it can be said to be, because the operation of such a doctrine of freedom as a cultural ideology is proving almost universally disastrous. And what makes the account even more persuasive is that, however paradoxical the Reformed view may appear to be, its paradox derives more from the complexities of the relation between God and his creatures than the paradox of its rival, which derives from the inherent contradictions of the liberal position.

III   *The double mistake of modern 'liberalism'*

In sum so far: modern liberalism fundamentally misconstrues the human condition, in both its createdness and its fallenness, confusing freedom and sin. A move to a re-establishment of a properly theological and Reformed doctrine of freedom will require at least the following. First, created freedom is not only compatible with, but actually requires constraint if it is to be genuinely a freedom of the creature. Jeremy Begbie has made the point with respect to music, that the freedom of improvisation is dependent on a high degree of cultural constraints, in this case 'the given musical material and strategies which shape it'.[25] Music, as the supremely temporal art, reminds us of the fact that we are shaped and formed in time, as the allusion above to *habitus* makes clear. Begbie cites a comment on Barth's conception of the moral agent to the effect that constraint here means not 'confinement' but 'specificity' or 'particular shape':

> At first blush, 'limitation' suggests 'confinement', whereas Barth means something closer to 'specificity' or 'particular shape'. The human creature is limited ... in the sense that it is not an indeterminate, quasi-infinite moral self; but its

[25] Jeremy Begbie, *Theology, Music and Time* (forthcoming, Cambridge: Cambridge University Press, 2000).

limitedness by God is not its being hemmed in by an alien will, but rather its formation into *this* good creature.[26]

Limitation is a blessing, not a curse, and to evade it is to turn freedom into slavery. The material bodies in which we are born move inexorably to death, and it is what happens to and is made of that embodiedness which determines who and what we are, not some intellect and will which are somehow separate from and above them. (That is not to suggest that intellect and will do not transcend the constraints in any way; the problem with what for the sake of argument I am describing as liberalism is that it abstracts, or attempts to abstract, this transcendence from concrete material entanglements.) Similar considerations apply to our spatiality, with especial reference to the limitations of our knowledge which are referred to in the citation from Christoph Schwöbel above. It is important to reiterate that this is not in itself a curse but a blessing. Human createdness and particularity are the gifts of God, and liberate us to be the particular selves, the particular men and women, we are, children of particular parents and bound up with particular family, friends, colleagues and above all fellow members of the body of Christ, aspects of whose human journey we have been elected to share. To need to be God, to have to make ourselves, is not a freedom, but a terrible slavery, as our world is discovering to its cost. As tradition- and community-dwelling beings we have the accumulated wisdom of the ages and the love of our various fellow men and women on which to call, and this is liberating because it is what it means to be human. But there is a darker side, and to this we turn.

Second, being sinful human beings means, as we have seen, being entrapped in social arrangements and bodies which bear the marks of a deep and inherited corruption, handed on inexorably from generation to generation. If it is not the case, as is sometimes claimed, that the doctrine of original sin is the one demonstrable article of Christian belief – not because the relation to God which determines it is not demonstrable – then something like it is. As we have seen, it is a mark of Kant's greatness that even this believer in the absoluteness of human

[26] John B. Webster, *Barth's Ethics of Reconciliation* (Cambridge: Cambridge University Press, 1995), p. 71.

freedom held that moral optimism was in face of the actual facts an absurdity. It follows that there is freedom for the human moral agent only in being set free. 'Where the Spirit of the Lord is, there is freedom' (2 Cor. 3.17), clearly means in its context that only through reconciliation with God the Father through the substitutionary death of his incarnate Son Jesus is the proper human particularity – right relation to God, the neighbour and the world – restored by reorientation to the eschatological perfection that is the promise of human being in the world. It is in this light only that we return to the theology of the glory of God, something, it is to be noted, highly prominent in the passage from 2 Corinthians that has formed the background to the theology of this paragraph.

IV *A defence of the* Soli Dei Gloria

As has already been at least implicitly suggested, it is a mistake to use the doctrine of the image of God in such a way that there is a univocal transference of attributes from God to the human being. To say that the freedom of the human being is only freedom if it is undetermined is in effect to apply a particular concept of divine freedom uncritically to the human case. (We might even ask whether the attribution of an essentially Ockhamist concept of freedom as absolute self-determination to God ignores the fact that God the Father's act is determined by the fact that he is the Father of the Son in the communion of the Holy Spirit; as we have seen Calvin saying, God is necessarily unable to do evil and so not *absolutely* free.) For example, one of the most foolish theological *dicta* ever to be uttered and given wide currency by vain repetition is that, 'if God is male, then the male is God'. It is both logically inconsequential and theologically false. Quite apart from the dubious assumption implicit in the hypothetical, it is by no means evident that the consequent in any case follows.

In our context, the conclusion is to be drawn that divine self-glorification may be considered to be legitimate in a way that human self-glorification is not. (I say 'may' because we have not yet discussed what form such self-glorification may and may not take.) Steve Holmes makes a similar point with reference to

Edwards. 'In *Two Dissertations*, which he left on his desk when he died, Edwards made the point: only God can be God without becoming demonic.'[27] Here I refer again to Miroslav Volf's point about violence. It by no means follows that the conceivability of divine (eschatological) violence undermines the validity of an ethic of non-violence.[28] We must hold on to this if we are not to minimize the seriousness of sin and evil by sentimentalizing God's way of dealing with it, which is by the cross. The two aspects of our topic come together in the judgement, first, that human self-glorification is the root of sin because it is precisely that which ignores and therefore distorts and disrupts the teleology and so the *being* of the created order. Calvin was not so wrong in characterising sin as pride because it is in pride that human beings aspire to being that which they are not created to be. Barth's point about the root of all sin – that 'man wants to be his own judge', is to the same effect.[29] To grasp at human glory is to exchange the glory of God for a lie.

The heart of human sin is that it is self-centred and individualistic. Might it not appear that this is the case with God, also? On some conceptions that would indeed be a justified charge.

> On the basis of a unipersonalist understanding of God the statement [sc. that creation exists to glorify God] would indeed come close to theological catastrophe. It is here that the understanding of God as the triune Creator introduces quite a different perspective ... [O]n the basis of a trinitarian understanding of God, glory is not a self-directed activity, but the mutuality of glorifying the other and receiving glory from the other which constitutes the communion of the divine life. Trinitarian glory is communicating glory and communicated glory.[30]

We now come to a second point. On a trinitarian understanding, there is not, in God's case as there is in the human, a

[27] Steve Holmes, 'Edwards on the Will', *International Journal of Systematic Theology* 1 (1999), 266–85, p. 273.

[28] See above, note 9.

[29] Barth, *Church Dogmatics* 4/1, p. 220.

[30] Christoph Schwöbel, 'God, Creation and the Christian Community', *The Doctrine of Creation*, edited by Colin E. Gunton (Edinburgh, T. & T. Clark), pp. 149–76, p. 169.

contradiction between the seeking of glory and the love of the
other. God's actions in the world, as the overflow of his eternal
triune glory into the order of time and space, are intrinsically
other-directed. 'Father, the hour has come. Glorify your Son,
that the Son may glorify you' (John 17.1). It is of the essence of
the three persons of the Trinity that they give glory to one
another, and what is true of the eternal being of God is also the
case with the divine actions *ad extra*. The full scope of this inner
glory which overflows outwards into the world is shown in
Barth's summary of the *gloria Dei* of which he read in the works
of Petrus van Mastricht, who 'alone among the Reformed
orthodox attempted a detailed examination and presentation
of the concept ... in a way which does justice to all the biblical
statements and references':

> the glorification which God prepares for Himself by His
> being within the Godhead; the glorification of the Son by the
> Father and of the Father by the Son; the glorification of God
> as it may and should be offered by angels and men; His glori-
> fication in His Word, in the Gospel, in Jesus Christ Himself;
> His glorification in the works of the creation, preservation
> and overruling of the world, and especially in the miracles of
> the history of revelation; His glorification in His grace
> granted to the Church and in the secrets of its ways and
> constitution.[31]

By what means does God glorify himself in the economy of his
acts towards and in the world? Not only, we must say, by the
weakness of the cross, but by the whole economy of creation,
reconciliation and redemption: that is to say, in the beginning,
middle and end of God's acts towards and in the order of time
and space, as its creator, redeemer and perfecter. The way in
which, however, we construe that is determinative of the way we
conceive of God's glory. First, we must say that the glory of God
is simply what the creation is for. It is created *in order to* return
God's goodness and giving in joyful praise, praise of words,
works and life. That God glories in this praise of his creatures is
in itself no more objectionable than that an orchestra glories in
the applause of its audience. Irenaeus's much cited saying that

---

[31] Barth, *Church Dogmatics* 2/1 p. 649.

'the glory of God is a human being truly alive' is here very much to the point.[32] But, second, as we have seen, apart from reconciliation with the creator, there is only death – unfreedom consisting in a slavery to that which is not God, by virtue of sin. Reconciliation is at the heart, because there the false exchange (Romans 1) is displaced by the 'blessed exchange' of the cross, as, for example, the argument of the Letter to the Ephesians makes manifest. Similarly, when John's Jesus speaks of his 'lifting up' or glorification reference is made to the cross, but also to the whole gamut of action and passion by which Jesus moves from the incarnation of the eternal Word to his ascension and mediation of the life-giving Spirit. One could here cite Ephesians 1.3–10 *in extenso*. God is praised, given glory, because he has chosen his people, both Jew and Gentile, to serve his purpose, realised in the blood of the cross, finally 'to bring all things in heaven and on earth together under one head, even Christ' (Eph. 1.10). It follows that freedom is an eschatological concept, realisable only where the Spirit brings people and things into right relation with God – and that does not mean exclusively 'the believers' – as we have seen Calvin affirming. 'The Lord is the Spirit, and where the Spirit of the Lord is there is freedom.'

The paradox of anthropocentrism is that that which seeks human glory denies both it and God's. 'In the mystery of God's providence, those who do seek the kingdom find that various other flourishings often follow, but not when directly aimed at.'[33] Is it not the case that the quality of Bach's music, as music, is enhanced by the fact that it was written to the glory of God, that of some pretentious modern humanistic mirror images, Strauss's *Also Sprach Zarathustra* for example,[34] diminished *as music* because it displaces the praise that is due to God alone? Perhaps Forsyth's attack on modern anthropocentrism is even more to the point: 'There is even what we might call a racial egotism, a self-engrossment of mankind with itself, a naive and tacit assumption that God were no God if he cared for anything

[32] Irenaeus, *Against the Heresies* 4. 20. 7. Gloria dei vivens homo; vita autem hominis visio dei.

[33] Plantinga, *Breviary*, p. 38.

[34] On British television, appropriately chosen to accompany broadcasting of one of the most futile of modern enterprises, the landing on the moon.

more than he did for his creatures.'[35] In sum: it is where the gospel flies in the face of what is dearest to modernity's heart that we find the very place where the modern world might find its most wholesome and edifying lesson. But let the last word be with the poet:

> He that to praise and laud thee doth refrain,
> Doth not refrain unto himself alone,
> But robs a thousand who would praise thee fain,
> And doth commit a world of sinne in one.[36]

---

[35] P. T. Forsyth, *The Person and Place of Jesus Christ* (London: Independent Press, 1946), p. 11. I thank Justyn Terry for this reference.
[36] George Herbert, 'Providence'.

CHAPTER 10

GOD, GRACE AND FREEDOM[1]

I *Varieties of freedom*

If one were to place on a spectrum the different theories of human freedom which have appeared in the history of thought, the two ends would be represented by, on the one hand, modern theories of the absolute void, and, on the other, highly deterministic views like that of Spinoza that freedom consists in the resigned recognition of complete determination. At one end, theories of the void see willed choice as absolute: an action is not free unless it is entirely within the undetermined choice of the agent. Insofar as it is determined by social context, education, tradition or anything other than the undetermined will of the agent, thus far it is not free. Such a conception of freedom necessarily serves chiefly as an ideal, although something like it appears in a number of modern writings, as scarcely needs pointing. Indeed, it is clear that the modern idea of freedom as a void, an empty space in which an agent affects to operate with complete freedom of choice, derives from the rejection of God, as, for example, it takes shape in one of the fathers of void theory, Friedrich Nietzsche. Freedom is only truly freedom when the agent creates, *ex nihilo*, the form of action which is adopted. To trace the conception a little further back, and to its motivating power, we can see in Hegel's theory of the unhappy consciousness the development of a view that to submit to the other, especially to the omnipotent other, is a denial of essential humanity. It is accordingly in the context of

[1] First published in *God and Freedom: Essays in Historical and Systematic Theology*, edited for the Research Institute in Systematic Theology by Colin E. Gunton (Edinburgh: T. & T. Clark, 1995), pp. 119–33.

the modern rejection of God that freedom becomes the assertion of the self in face of that which would deprive of freedom. And because to reject God is in effect to reject any metaphysical context or matrix for human freedom, the void is ultimately all that remains.

At the other end of the spectrum, theories of more or less absolute determinism are also to be found, although in practice, I suspect, also mainly as ideals: for example, ideals of total scientific explanation which will in principle predict all future actions on the basis of the knowledge of present and past. Underlying such ideals in the modern age is the mechanistic theory of the universe, now apparently on its deathbed, but effectively still encouraging the scientism that would affect to explain every action as the necessary outcome of the previous state of the universe. That, too, is a highly damaging theory, in depriving moral agents of that which seems to make them moral agents, their freedom to have done otherwise, and on which most notions of personality and responsibility depend. But it is characteristic of the kind of concept that fills the vacuum left by the loss of the concept of God in modern thought. Nature or evolution or the universe become the hypostatized agents from which everything derives, as by necessity. The pantheistic undertones of such theories are obvious.

The two ends of the spectrum, absolute freedom and absolute determinism, are notable for the fact that they tend to turn into one another. The response to scientific determinism is often an advocacy of the ethics of the void – as in Jacques Monod[2] – while the vacuum left by the void is often filled by some form of political authoritarianism, as Edward Craig has pointed out:

> Quite apart from the instability of the world which it might easily encourage, it is psychologically unstable in itself. It is the philosophy of the confident man, or, as its opponents would very likely have it, the over-confident man. Should that confidence flag it offers no secure consolation. The image of the void, from being a symbol of the limitless liberty of the

[2] Jacques Monod, *Chance and Necessity. An Essay in the Natural Philosophy of Modern Biology*, translated by Austryn Wainhouse (London: Collins, 1972).

agent, becomes a menacing abyss waiting to engulf all his purposes and reduce him to a nullity.[3]

Accordingly, neither extreme, the one a denial of our rootedness in the material universe, the other a denial of our personal transcendence of it, can be finally satisfying, for reasons that will appear below.

Most theories of freedom would appear to lie somewhere between the two poles represented by absolute freedom and absolute determinism. In the writings of post-war analytic philosophy there are to be found debates about whether, and in what way, freedom and determinism might be supposed to be compatible. For the most part, such attempts are based on the assumption that what I have called poles or the ends of a spectrum are the fundamental possibilities, and have in some way to be reconciled. Their background, too, is, fairly clearly, to be found in a deterministic view of the world culled from mechanist theories of science. And they bring me to a first major point. The theories I have reviewed depend upon a particular view of the moral agent as subsisting in some form of unmediated relation to the universe, and it is that which in this chapter I wish to contest. They share an implausible conception of the fully formed individual consciousness, will or reason either facing or being swallowed by the totally other universe – or some dialectic of the two. Such a dualistic picture is fundamentally unsatisfactory at whatever level it is considered because it ignores the webs of relation in which agents are necessarily involved. What will serve to make the whole debate different is the search for mediating factors which show the implausibility of what remains in many modern discussions the paradigm view of freedom.

Once we concede that freedom is not an absolute – an absolute qualification of or absolute absence from the individual human agent – we shall realise a measure of mediation is necessarily involved. Freedom is not an immediate but a mediated relation to other people and to that world which is the realm and object of free human action. Our freedom does not come neat, but is in part mediated to us by

[3] Edward Craig, *The Mind of God and the Works of Man* (Oxford: Clarendon Press, 1987), p. 271.

our fellow human beings and by God. The place on the spectrum of any theory between the void and absolute determinism will therefore be determined by the weight and nature of the mediation: by the way in which we conceive that our being particularly ourselves is dependent upon the mediation of the Other or others. Thus the spectrum of theories will contain a wide range of positions that take their distinctive character from the nature of the mediation that is envisaged. Unlike the extreme positions, they are not based on the supposition that it is a simple matter of deciding how far I can escape from or in some way evade determination by the universe by asserting my independence. The quest is for freedom as a relational category. At the centre of the question of mediation is the personal dimension, although even here our relation to the material universe is not irrelevant. For the purposes of this chapter, however, under consideration is the contention that what it is to be a free human being is bound up with our relations with other personal beings, and it is that especially which widens the range of possibilities beyond the extremes of determinism and the void. That is why even the supposedly most extreme versions of the Augustinian or Reformed positions – those of Augustine himself, Calvin and Jonathan Edwards, for example – are not absolute determinisms of the scientistic kind, because they involve the interposition of some form of personal agency. And that is where the question of grace enters the debate.

II *Mediated freedom*

Two main theses are to be argued in the remainder of the chapter. First is that freedom, before it is conceived as free or undetermined choice or willing, should be conceived in terms of, as a function of, personal particularity. In such a reformulation of the question, all the traditional foreground characteristics of freedom remain important: self-determination, moral responsibility and the rest. But without some prior consideration of what kind of beings make choices and behave responsibly or irresponsibly, their meaning hangs in the air. So that, adapting or misusing Luther, I would propound the following pair of theses:

1. Freedom is that which I do with my own particularity, that which enables me to be myself and do what is truly and distinctively mine.
2 Freedom is that which others do to and with my particular being, in enabling me to be and do, or preventing me from being and doing, that which is particularly myself.

To make the first claim is to say that to be free is to realise what one distinctively and particularly is. To make the second is not to deny it, any more than Luther's second statement that the Christian is the servant of all is to deny his first that the Christian is the free lord of all. It is to expand the meaning of the first, and to say that one's self-realisation, one's freedom, is something that depends integrally and not merely contingently upon one's relation to the other.

The claim can be illustrated quite simply. If you incarcerate me, either literally or metaphorically in, for example, an intolerably adversarial professional relation, then you thus far deprive me of being myself.[4] Freedom is a relational concept in the sense that it cannot be understood merely individualistically. If we are free, it is in large measure because others enable or empower us to be free. Freedom may be something that we exercise or fail to exercise as particular beings, but our particularity is at the same time something that comes to us from the other beings with whom we are related. That point requires to be stressed strongly because it flies in the face not only of the fashions of the age, which tend to see the person as the individual engaged on a quest for self-fulfilment, a conception definitively questioned in recent times by Charles Taylor,[5] but also of the individualist assumptions of much of the Christian tradition's theologies of grace and justification, which sometimes appear to present the relation between the individual soul and God as the only significant one.

Before, however, that first thesis can be developed, the question of the relation of God and human freedom must be

---

[4] We might want to say that the latter is worse, because it is our relations with others that so determine what we are severally able to become, but that is not the matter with which I am concerned at this stage.

[5] Charles Taylor, *Sources of the Self. The Making of the Modern Identity* (Cambridge: Cambridge University Press, 1989).

engaged. And here it must be said – and this is the second major thesis – that whatever the failures of the tradition, it is right in its fundamental contention that the prior mediating factor of human freedom is the relation to God. The fact that we are creatures and not creators of ourselves, as void theories imply, means that our relation to God is determinative not only for who and what we are, but for how we conceive that freedom of which we are speaking. That is a point which is neglected in many of the discussions to which I have alluded, partly for the reason already mentioned, that modern theories often presuppose the necessity of rejecting God, or at least of supposing him to be minimally relevant to the question. But once the God-relationship is thrown into the ring, there is no question but that it will have a major bearing upon this question, as upon any other. The complexity of the topic of freedom arises therefore not from the dialectic of void and determinism but from the fact that because there are many competing, or at least diverse, accounts of the human relationship to God, there are also many ways of answering the questions of what human freedom is and of the respects in which it exists.

The human relation to God must be understood on two levels, the second of which will be the chief concern of this chapter. The first level concerns the doctrine of sin. The claim of the mainstream Augustinian and Reformation teaching is that, in point of fact, the condition of the person apart from grace is not one of freedom, but of slavery, and, to boot, a largely self-imposed slavery. If we are to come to terms with the human condition, we cannot evade the almost self-evident truth of the doctrine of sin. The misuse of freedom renders the agent in certain major respects unfree, a slave to self and to necessity. In support of that thesis I can call such diverse figures as Paul, John, Augustine, Anselm, Luther, Calvin, Kant – in certain aspects of his moral theory – Coleridge, Barth and Niebuhr. That said, there are rival accounts of how the lost freedom is to be granted or restored. The inconsistencies of Kant's view, which is the chief rival today to the Augustinian-Reformed account, have been the subject of two recent studies, and it is worth while pausing to look at them because of the light they throw on both levels of the human relation to God.

Gordon Michalson's achievement in *Fallen Freedom* is to elucidate the contradiction at the heart of Kant's *Religion within the Limits of Reason Alone*. He shows that the disturbing element, both in that book and in relation to Kant's philosophy of autonomy in general, is the concept of radical evil. Here Kant comes very near to the traditional Christian doctrine of original sin, teaching that 'Radical evil is "innate" but "brought upon us" by our own freedom.'[6] Again in correspondence with the Christian tradition Kant has a doctrine of moral regeneration, but this clashes with what Michalson rightly takes to be 'close to being the animating center of Kant's entire philosophical anthropology', 'the idea that we "make ourselves"'.[7] How does Kant escape the corner into which he has painted himself? According to Michalson, by adopting a theory of dual perspective. By looking at things from the perspectives of both eternity and time, the divine and the human, Kant purports to achieve a theory of salvation by grace which is in no way contrary to his theory of autonomy. But, particularly in view of his Newtonian determinism, he cannot:

> Kant tries valiantly to translate [his] appeals to divine action into commentary on the psychology of the moral agent ... If he eliminates the vagueness and becomes more blunt in these appeals, Kant unduly compromises both the rationalism of his basic position and the integrity of his fundamentally mechanistic outlook. But without these appeals, he runs the even greater risk of leaving the moral agent in defeat and despair.[8]

Kant wants a theology of grace, but is prevented from achieving it for philosophical reasons. His relation to the Western Christian tradition's theology of grace is therefore a dialectical one. On the one hand, he rejects it in the name of autonomy, but is too clear-eyed about the human condition to reject it *in toto*. On the other, he is in continuity with that tradition in attempting to reconcile Platonic and Hebraic strands in moral

---

[6] Gordon E. Michalson, Jr., *Fallen Freedom. Kant on Radical Evil and Moral Regeneration* (Cambridge: Cambridge University Press, 1990), p. 8.

[7] Michalson, *Fallen Freedom*, p. 38.

[8] Michalson, *Fallen Freedom*, p. 128.

philosophy. As we shall see, earlier attempts to develop a theology of grace similarly fail to achieve a satisfactory synthesis.

But before we conclude this section, it is worthwhile pausing to outline another recent study of Kant which casts a rather different light on his moral philosophy. *Grace and Law* is a study of Paul's moral philosophy by a Jewish specialist in the thought of Aristotle and Kant. Heinz Cassirer's fundamental contention is that, even leaving aside Paul's teaching on grace, his analysis of the human plight is more convincing than Kant's. Central to his argument is the contention of the insufficiency of the rationalism and dualism of reason and sense that Kant simply presupposes. '[I]f the correctness of this assumption be called in question – as it surely must be – it is found ... that Kant has no other argument at his disposal to support his assertion that man's reasoning power is responsible for his consciousness of moral obligation.'[9] Cassirer proceeds to argue that In *Religion within the Limits of Reason Alone* Kant modifies and strengthens his thesis, and thus sharpens the contention between himself and Paul, so that 'the point at issue between them is not the facts of the case but the manner in which they are dealt with'.[10] Here Paul is right, Kant wrong: 'only a love as overpowering and ever-abiding as the one he describes will ever be capable of remedying so deep seated a malady.'[11] The conclusion is inescapable. The failure of the Kantian account of salvation means either that the human condition is beyond help or that the Augustinian-Reformed position is right. Without grace taking shape in atonement, without, that is to say, the mediation of Christ, human freedom must be understood to be at best curtailed, at worst virtually ineffective. Cassirer concludes that Paul's statement is therefore definitive: 'by the grace of God I am what I am' (1 Cor. 15.10). But in coming to this conclusion and working out its implications we must remain aware that, for some good reasons, the modern mind finds it unacceptable. 'So long as one remains within the Kantian orbit, one is committed to the view that giving the principle of divine grace admittance into the moral life of man

[9] Heinz Cassirer, *Grace and Law. St. Paul, Kant and the Hebrew Prophets* (Grand Rapids: Eerdmans, 1988), p. 64.
[10] Cassirer, *Grace and Law*, p. 82.
[11] Cassirer, *Grace and Law*, p. 28.

must have the effect of degrading man and depriving him of his dignity.'[12]

This consideration must be kept in mind as we come to the second and, for our purposes, the crucial level at which the human relation to God must be understood. Suppose that in some way or other there does take place in Christ a restoration of that relationship to God without which there is no true human freedom. What is its form in the present? Does freedom have to be mediated continually, or is it, once given, an absolute and disposable possession, like some form of gnostic enlightenment? The traditional answer is that the continuing relationship too has something to do with grace, not the grace of atonement, but the grace by which some continuing form of authentic human action is made possible without depriving the agent of freedom. People like to speak in this connection of a dialectic, calling on that part of Paul's verse which was not cited above: 'I worked harder than any of them, though it was not I, but the grace of God which is with me.' Paul's actions are his own, but in a sense they are not. That is what D. M. Baillie famously called the paradox of grace, a paradox transmitted to the Western tradition by Augustine.[13] But what is this grace? Are we truly concerned with paradox and dialectic, or can some more systematically satisfying account be given of freedom in relation to grace? They are the questions that must concern us as we pursue the question of the mediation of freedom.

III   *Grace*

Divine grace is better understood as a mode of God's action towards or relatedness to the creature than as some kind of substance that God imparts to the creature. For that reason there is much to be said for P. T. Forsyth's famous objection to the expression in Newman's hymn, 'a higher gift than grace'. There can be no higher gift than grace if grace means a form of God's relatedness to us. If that is so, it would also seem right

---

[12] Cassirer, *Grace and Law*, p. 82.

[13] D. M. Baillie, *God Was in Christ. An Essay on Incarnation and Atonement* (London: Faber, 1961), pp. 114–15.

to say that the relationship of God to Adam and Eve in Genesis 2, before the Fall, is a gracious one, or with Rahner that all creaturely existence is in some way graced existence.[14] Grace is not something reserved for sinners, we might say, but the fundamental form of God's relation to the creature. But, as we have seen, the question of grace takes its most interesting shape in connection with the free human action that is supposedly mediated by it to those set free from a state of unfreedom. Is that grace rightly described as 'it'? The problem with much traditional treatment, I can suggest without claiming originality, is that grace has so often been reified, turned into a thing, so that the mediator of divine action is effectively conceived of in impersonal, or, perhaps more accurately, only quasi-personal terms. Let us examine some of the problems before turning to examine the form of divine action in relation to the creature with which we are concerned.

The notion of grace as a way of understanding the mediation of divine action in such a way that human freedom is maintained is crucial to the Western tradition, and absolutely necessary if we are to avoid both the extreme concepts of freedom I have sketched and the various Pelagianising forms of theology that have arisen in their light. We can share with those who would distinguish between uncreated and created grace a concern to maintain the mediatedness of all divine action, at least in one sense of the word mediation. For the same reason we should also beware of all conceptions of direct divine action on the person or the soul, as in some of the ideas which Augustine explores and as in some forms of mysticism. The absolute dependence on God of any person or action may take away the very freedom which we are seeking to validate theologically, and indeed the heart of modern protest atheism and the quest for the void can be understood as a rebellion against forms of divine action which are not gracious.[15]

But what is meant by this distinction between mediated and immediate forms of divine action towards the world and the

[14] To say that is not to accept the form that Rahner's theology of grace takes.
[15] That is the reason why apparently the same mode of response to God may be construed very differently by those with different theologies of grace. Thus the calls to obedience on the part of a Bonhoeffer and, say, an advocate of political authoritarianism will be construed very differently.

moral agent? It is not designed completely to avoid the notion
of direct divine action, as if God is dualistically divided from
the world and can act only through a hierarchy of being, of the
kind presupposed in Aquinas's Five Ways, so that action at a
lower level is always mediated by action at a higher, and
ultimately by God.[16] On this kind of understanding, God
operates directly on the soul, indirectly on lower forms of
being, sometimes by means of secondary causes. It is not that
essentially Platonizing kind of mediation with which I am
concerned. According to Irenaeus, divine action in and towards
the world takes place through the action of the Father's two
hands, the Son and the Spirit. According to such a conception,
God acts mediately but directly. For christological reasons in
particular we know that there is no need of a hierarchy of
agency, because here we recognise the freedom of God to
involve himself directly in the material world. This is important
for our purposes for two reasons in particular. First, the
concept of grace as a kind of insubstantial substance took
the shape that it did because of a dualistic and christologically
deficient conception of the mediation of divine action. Thus
many Western conceptions of grace appear to *replace* christologically conceived divine action in and towards the world.
Second, the concept of grace as a kind of mediating substance
similarly displaces the notion of the action of God the Spirit, as
Robert Jenson has argued in his treatise on the Spirit. The
conceptual framework within which Pauline theology was
developed in Augustine and Aquinas, he argues, caused the
matter to be couched in terms of causal relations between
substances – to be sure, personal substances – so that what Paul
called the fruits of the Spirit came to be described as 'effects'.
'(T)his ineluctably sets the problem of the co-operation
between the graceful God and the ... graced creature. The
problem has been the crux of all Western theology.'[17]

   If, in face of this, we rather concentrate on a verbal – or
perhaps adverbial – rather than substantial conception of
grace; that is to say, if we conceive grace as a function of divine

---

[16] Anthony Kenny, *The Five Ways* (London: Routledge, 1969), pp. 41–5.
[17] Robert Jenson, 'The Holy Spirit', *Christian Dogmatics*, edited by C. E.
Braaten and R. W. Jenson (Philadelphia: Fortress Press, 1984), vol. 2, pp. 126f.

action in relation to the world, rather than as something thing-like, much is gained. In particular, grace will be understood to characterise the modes of God's action in both Son and Spirit. Thus, speaking christologically, we can say that the grace of God *is* the action of God in Christ confronting sin and evil with a particular form of action, namely that paradigmatically shown in the death of Jesus on the cross, but also in all the ministry of Jesus. That action has the content of a historic liberation from sin by forgiveness and reconciliation, once and for all. But this christologically mediated form of gracious action is not restricted to past-historic instances, but also has a bearing on our topic of continuing gracious and liberating divine action. The Letter to the Hebrews also, for example, is much concerned with the gracious action of God the Father mediated in the present by the ascended Christ. But, as I am chiefly concerned in this chapter with the continuing realisation, by divine action, of free human action, it will profit me to concentrate on the pneumatological dimensions of the matter, for it is where the Spirit is that there is liberty. Therefore the definition of grace can be expanded. By the grace of God is meant the gracious action towards the creature of God the Father, mediated by the Spirit through the Son. Put otherwise, we can say that by relating human beings to the Father through the Son, the Spirit is the one who graciously liberates people and things to be themselves. We must now explore how this notion of grace as the liberating action of the Spirit can take shape anthropologically and ecclesiologically.

IV   *Grace, freedom and particularity*

There has been in recent theology a measure of play with the notion of Jesus as a model for human freedom, though this has often been conceived moralistically, in a rather Pelagian manner, rather than in terms of grace. One exception is, of course, Karl Barth, though the suspicion in his case must be that there is a tendency in the opposite direction, to conceive the relation of God to the human Jesus in terms of the kind of unmediated relation with which this chapter is taking issue. His Christ, it might be said, demonstrates the freedom of God more successfully than the freedom of man. We therefore turn to Anselm of Canterbury for an approach to what must on almost any account be the crucial question for a theology of grace and freedom: what is the relation of the human Jesus to the God who directed to his death a moral agent who manifested a measure of reluctance in obeying the divine command? What kind of freedom do we see in the response of Jesus to the requirement that he die on the cross? The answer for Anselm is to be found in a characteristically Augustinian conception of freedom. His concern is to do justice both to the many scriptural texts showing that the cross was willed by the Father, and so a requirement of obedience by Jesus, and those that witness his free acceptance of the burden.

In his treatment of the question, Anselm assumes what cannot be assumed in the modern world, a rather authoritarian view of the human relation to God, that 'God requires (the upholding of truth and justice) from every rational creature, and that the latter owes this to God as a matter of obedience'.[18] To interpret Anselm rather freely, we might say that on this account the obedience of the cross was the *particular* form that Jesus' free obedience took. It was, to use the definition of freedom being used in this chapter, that which he did with his own particularity; that which enabled him to be and do what was truly and distinctively his action. 'Christ himself freely underwent death, not by yielding up his life as an act of obedience, but on account of his obedience in maintaining justice, because he so steadfastly persevered in it that he brought death on himself.'[19] A distinction is therefore to be drawn between mere obedience, a form of compulsion of the agent by God, and the obedience that takes the form of faithfully carrying out that which is the agent's particular form of just behaviour. It leads Anselm to a statement of the compatibility of obedience and freedom. 'For this is simple and true

---

[18] Anselm, *Cur Deus Homo* I. ix, translated by E. R. Fairweather, *Why God became Man, A Scholastic Miscellany: Anselm to Ockham*, Library of Christian Classics vol. 10 (London: SCM Press, 1956) p. 112. However apparently unmodern this is, we should be aware of the fact that, *mutatis mutandis*, it would be a view of the human condition shared by a number of modern political theologies.

[19] Anselm, *Why God became Man*, p. 113.

obedience, when the rational nature, not of necessity, but willingly keeps the will that it has received from God.'[20]

Anselm's treatment provides the parameters for a development of our topic, but, typically of the Western tradition, lacks an appreciation of the pneumatological dimension of the matter, perhaps because, as Jenson remarks of Augustine in this context, that tradition on the whole tends to treat the three persons of the Trinity as functionally indistinguishable.[21] But if we are to extricate ourselves from a causal understanding of grace as a quasi-substance bringing about certain effects, the functional distinction of the persons is precisely what is required. If Jesus is able freely to do that which is his particular calling, is not the mediator of that calling best understood to be the Holy Spirit, who mediates to him the Father's will, while – graciously – respecting his authentic humanity? Where the Spirit of the Lord is, there is freedom' (2 Cor. 3.17). On this account, to say that moral agents are enabled by grace freely to do something is to say that they are enabled by the Spirit's action to do that which is the particular form of action appropriate to them in the present. (It must be acknowledged here that this grace sometimes takes the form, though not in the case of Jesus, if not of coercion, at least of unwilled and often unwanted divine pressure. Under the conditions of fallenness, that will perhaps necessarily be the case, as is illustrated by the call of Jeremiah and Jonah, the conversion of Paul and the events making possible the writing of Francis Thompson's *The Hound of Heaven*. Does God coerce into freedom? In these cases, very nearly, it must appear.)

In the case of Jesus, then, freedom to be and do what is particularly his is mediated by the Spirit. But to remain there for our model of human freedom would be to forget the fact that our freedom takes shape in webs of human relationality. There is a horizontal as well as a vertical mediatedness to be taken into account. It was argued above, in the second of the adaptations of Luther, that freedom is that which others do to and with my particular being, in enabling me to be and do or preventing me from being and doing that which is particularly myself. One's

---

[20] Anselm, *Why God became Man*, p. 116.
[21] Robert W. Jenson, 'The Holy Spirit', p. 126.

self-realisation, one's freedom, is something that depends integrally and not merely contingently upon one's relation to the other. And that brings us to ecclesiology, by which is meant not merely the theology of the Church in particular but also a general theology of human being in community; what Daniel Hardy has called created sociality.[22] But it is through biblical ecclesiology that I shall approach the matter.

In the earlier part of this section, something was made of the characteristic mode of action of the Spirit as mediating freedom to the moral agent, illustrated as that was by his relationship to Jesus. It is surely significant that in the New Testament, the Spirit is also characteristically presented as the mediator of life in community. If one way of understanding sin is as enslavement to alienating patterns of relations, freedom correspondingly consists in the constitution of, or liberation to, patterns of relationality in which one's true being is realised. As we have seen, the determinative false relation is the vertical one, with God, so that the corresponding freedom is the freedom to be and do that which we are given by Christ and in the Spirit to be and to do. This freedom is realised by atonement and forgiveness. But it is not a shapeless freedom, freedom into a vacuum, which is given. Just as sin takes shape, as the opening chapters of Genesis show, in a range of personal and social dislocations, so salvation takes shape in a matrix of new and reconciled patterns of relations. One of the functions of ecclesiology, accordingly, is to provide an account of how it is that the Spirit gives freedom not merely individually, as in the classical understanding of the forgiveness of sins, but socially or in community.

But where does *grace* come in here? The answer is that if we are intrinsically relational beings, the grace – gracious action – of God is to be understood as that whereby he realises forms of relationality which can be described as free. By relating them to God in Christ, the Spirit at the same time and in the same act also relates the forgiven to one another. (That is the respect in which there is 'in Christ' no male or female, slave or free, etc.).

---

[22] Daniel W. Hardy, 'Created and Redeemed Sociality', *On Being the Church. Essays on the Christian Community*, edited by C. E. Gunton and D. W. Hardy (Edinburgh: T. & T. Clark, 1989), pp. 21–47.

The paradigm of this is to be found in the account of the sending of the Spirit in Acts 2, whose interpretation has long been obscured by a concentration on the signs and wonders in which the story is dressed. The centre of the story is not that but the realisation by the Spirit of community: community between the nations of earth symbolised by the reversal of Babel that is depicted, and community taking shape in the formation of the Church which is stressed so strongly as the outcome of what happened. But how can this be understood to take shape concretely in the present?

A true community – any true community – is one whose patterns of relationality enable its members to be, as members, distinctively and particularly themselves. Far too much stress has been placed in the tradition on the unity of the Church, which has for too much of her history both ecclesiastically and socially been the agent of homogeneity, at the expense of particularity and diversity. The interesting point here is that when the Pauline literature speaks of the Spirit in relation to the Church, it is at least as much interested in diversity as in unity: or rather, *it sees the latter as constituted by the former.* Notice how the following verses incorporate in a few words most of the themes of this discussion, and particularly the twofold mediation with which it has been concerned: 'Now there are varieties of gifts, but the same Spirit; and there are varieties of service, but the same Lord; and there are varieties of working, but it is the same God who inspires them all in every one' (1 Cor. 12.4–6). The point that should be stressed is that particularity is realised in community. But, and here we come to the link with the secondary features of freedom, it must be free community in the sense of being unconstrained and entered into voluntarily. It should not be suggested that freedom under grace, enabled by divine action, is not the exercise of the free human will. But it is a will whose direction is given shape by the patterns of relation in which it is set. It is not the freedom of empty space. Only in relation to God and to others can we be particularly who and what we are, and therefore only so can we be free.

There is a further point to be made. Freedom, it has been claimed, is something that is the expression of our particularity, albeit particularity in community. It is a gracious gift, of the

God who reconciles us to himself through his Son and relates us to others in saving ways by his Spirit. But because it is realised in community, we must understand it as a function of relationality also in that it is something that we receive from and give to one another. Grace is therefore something that marks liberating human action also, for it is a form of action in which others are enabled to be themselves. To be schematic: whereas in the modern age we tend naturally to conceive of freedom as freedom from the other, this picture assists us in thinking of freedom as for and (deriving) from the other.

There are dangers of idealisation in this picture. The way in which ecclesiastical life has taken shape historically has often submerged these aspects, though they are, I believe, authentically biblical. But although they have been submerged, they have not always been absent. What is to be hoped for in the light of all this is a change of priorities in ecclesiology, away from the two poles, individualistic and authoritarian, which are to some extent reflexes of one another, and towards an ecclesiology of the personal. And that brings us back to two of the major themes of the chapter. The first is the relation between concepts of grace and concepts of the Church. It was argued that previous doctrines of grace conceived as quasi-substantial tended to displace the personal, gracious, action of God the Father mediated by the Son and Spirit. There is a case for arguing that they have been contributors to the inadequate ecclesiologies, objective-institutional[23] and subjective-individualist, which have so disfigured the Christian centuries. In the former, grace is something channelled by the institution; in the latter, a function of the individual's direct experience. The notion of grace as a form of mediated divine action which *enables* gracious human action, and particularly action in community, should facilitate some correction of the weakness, and serve to obviate the necessity of choosing between an institutional and an individualistic approach to Christian community.

The second is the question of the relation between uncreated and created grace, which led to some of the unnecessary

---

[23] This is not to deny the values of institutionality, but lament the fact that it has taken forms which subvert rather than realise the personal.

complexities of mediaeval theology and helped to trigger the Reformation. The traditional form is stated by Aquinas: 'Grace may be understood in two ways: in one way as the divine aid that moves us to will and act well, in the other way as a divinely given dispositional quality.'[24] That is another form of the dualism that separates divine and human action rather than integrating them. According to the alternative being suggested here, uncreated grace is to be understood as the eternal gracious freedom of the love in which Father, Son and Spirit are from and for each other in eternity. God's being is eternally gracious because that is a way of characterising the reciprocal love of persons. This grace takes temporal form in the gracious ways towards us of the triune God, in the economy of creation and redemption mediated by the Son and the Spirit. 'Created grace' is correspondingly not a substance poured into us or in some way bringing about effects in our action, nor is it only a form of divine aid, but consists in forms of gracious action that are realised in the free human response to the gracious Spirit. Thus two desiderata of a theology of divine action are achieved. The first is the relatedness of God and the world, by virtue of which the creation is able to become what it is called to be by virtue only of God's creating and reconciling action. The second is what can be called the *space* between God and the world whereby God, by his action, enables the world to be truly itself. Such a relation in otherness of God and the creature was not adequately guaranteed by the old theory, but is opened up by the personal form of mediation here suggested and so allows for a shaped freedom other than that of the void. Moreover, because it is truly gracious, divine action towards the creature does not deprive the agent of personal integrity, but constitutes it in its freedom, and thus in turn makes possible gracious forms of human action. For is it not a defining mark of grace that it gives due place to the other, and therefore enables the other to be free?

---

[24] Aquinas, *Summa Theologiae*, 1a 2ae. 3. 2.

INDEX OF SUBJECTS

INDEX OF NAMES